THE
COACHING LIFE

THE
COACHING·LIFE

Harry Hanson

*Manchester
University Press*

Copyright © Harry Hanson 1983

First published 1983 by
Manchester University Press
Oxford Road, Manchester M13 9PL, UK
51 Washington Street, Dover, N.H. 03820, USA

British Library cataloguing in publication data

Hanson, Harry
 The coaching life
 1. Coaching — Great Britain — History
 I. Title
 388.3′228′0941   HE5749.G7

ISBN 0–7190–0930–8

Library of Congress cataloging in publication data

Hanson, Harry.
 The coaching life
 Includes bibliographical references and index.
 1. Coaching — Great Britain — History — 19th century.
2. Coaching — Ireland — History — 19th century.
3. Coaching — France — History — 19th century. I. Title.
HE5749.G7H36 1983   388.3′ 228′ 0941   83-11538
ISBN 0-7190-0930-8

Typeset in Hong Kong by
Graphicraft Typesetters Limited
Printed in Hong Kong
by Wing King Tong Co Ltd

CONTENTS

PREFACE

Books on coaching generally develop the story from the first
lumbering vehicles of the seventeenth century through highwaymen, boggy heaths and the torture of fourteen days from
London to Edinburgh . . . before coming to the 'perfection' of
the 1830s. There is usually a chapter on 'posting' — the
approved mode of travel of the wealthy, involving the hire of
horses (and carriages) from staged 'post houses' (usually inns),
ridden by aged postillions called 'post boys'.

Here, we pass over posting and the early days . . . to 1815,
when coaching begins to come to glory, and we can look more
closely at its heyday down to 1837 when Britain (and Ireland)
were criss-crossed by an efficient network of rapid coach services — with Edinburgh only forty-seven hours from London.
We step a little beyond to see its demise.

Nostalgia has coloured much previous literature, but the
dearth of business records makes detailed academic treatment
difficult. This book is not that long-awaited study. On the
contrary, it is anecdotal rather than analytical. But in con-
centrating on this brief period we can spare time to get behind
the romance of the road. A little space can be devoted to the
remarkable transport innovations wrought by the remarkable
Carlos Bianconi. We can look more seriously at deficiencies
usually ignored or humorously glossed over. And, for once, we
can compare Britain with other countries. Was it really 'the
most efficient system of land transportation the world had yet
seen?'

For help in preparing the book I am indebted to staffs of the
British Library and Newspaper Library at Colindale, the House

of Lords Record Office, the Public Record Office, the public libraries of Birmingham and Oxford and the Record Offices of Lancashire and Northamptonshire. Individuals who helped were Jenny Finklaire, Julia Holmes, Christine Ironfield, Mary Prior, Peter Sweetman and Rosa Young. The manuscript was typed, efficiently and cheerfully, by Anita Cook.

Illustrations are reproduced by courtesy of the *Banbury Guardian*, the Reference Library, Social Sciences Department, Birmingham Public Libraries, the British Library and Newspaper Library, British Railways Board, Mrs Julia Holmes, London Transport Museum and Oxford University Press. Despite enquiries I have not been able to trace the owner of copyright in the two pictures by George Wright (1860–1942) on pp. 18 and 112; the publishers would of course wish to make due acknowledgement.

For Armelle

1

PET AND DARLING OF
THE PEOPLE

At midday on 20 June 1815 John Fowler, proprietor of the White Hart, Aylesbury, was hay making behind the inn. Hearing his name, he turned to see the *Dairy Maid* London–Buckingham pair-horse coach beyond the hedge.

'Master John,' repeated Hodgkins, the coachman, 'I bring you great news, and no one in Aylesbury shall know it before you. Bonyparte and all his French army are destroyed! The Duke of Wellington — God bless him! — has fought and beat him at a place called Waterloo.'

Young Fowler, then twenty-three, overjoyed, fell on his knees to thank God for the blessing of peace, having lived all his life in time of war.

Hodgkins, with blue ribbons on the horses' heads, a big bow on his whip, drove triumphantly through the town, telling everyone the startling news.[1]

This short account sums up one reason why the coach was becoming 'pet and darling of the people'. As the network expanded and quickened it carried not only 'life and cheerfulness' to more and more towns and villages but news of great events.

William Bayzand, guard of the London–Hereford *Mazeppa* for many years, recalled the excitement in 1832 as the Reform Bill went through Parliament.

'Has the Bill passed?' he was asked a hundred times.

'Yes.'

'So, as we travelled down the road the interest became greater.'

Bayzand had augmented his stock of *Times* newspapers. 'At

Shottenham, a gentleman put a sovereign in my hand and took the *Times*. At Ross, the excitement ran much higher, for there I . . . received two sovereigns. I assure you, I put no price; the money was voluntarily given, and they seemed to be quite delighted.'

At Hereford, ' . . . before the coach had well stopped, I was on the shoulders of four men, carried to the Inn, and the price of the paper still kept rising. They gave me a £5 Hereford Old Bank note.'[2]

The guard of the Edinburgh mail had been less well received the year before, when the Bill failed. Over five thousand people awaited his arrival but, 'not being so communicative as the multitude desired, was rather roughly treated'.

Thousands gathered to await the mails at moments of great national excitement. In 1820 'along the line of the Mails crowds stood waiting in the burning sunshine for news of the trial' of Queen Caroline, but Thomas Lightfoot, in Carlisle gaol, equally eagerly awaited the mail's arrival in August 1820 for a different reason. The hoped-for news never came, and he was duly executed. Viall, awaiting execution in Bury in 1829, was luckier — but not by much. 'This morning the mail con-

Arrival of the London mail, Bristol, 1826. *British Library*

veyed respite for this culprit during Royal pleasure. This is tantamount to an order for confinement as a lunatic.'[3]

Even on a normal day the London mail drew a sizeable crowd. It arrived in Bristol, for example, at 10 a.m. and there was 'always. a great anxiety to obtain the London news and price current, so much so that, the leading merchants and others, assemble in front of the Post Office ... to wait the arrival of the letters of advice which are to regulate their concerns'.[4] It was the same wherever it passed. The guard was a 'certificated newsmonger ... What he said was absolute, there was no time for argument, and the few words which he addressed to the customary group afforded matter for the smoking room for a whole evening.'[5]

The vicar of Tadcaster had a shock when the Edinburgh mail sped through, horn blaring, sporting a huge black flag. Certain that the monarch at least was dead, he rode after the coach to discover that Mundig, whose jockey's colours were black, had won the Derby. Not everyone appreciated such news-bearing. Another cleric aboard a Lancashire mail got no rest because all night the guard was roaring out, 'The Cure.' It turned out that horse had won the Champagne Stakes.[6]

Coaches also carried news of any serious criminal offence and were often the means of detection. This was especially so in cases of horse stealing, as coach crews usually noticed horses along the road, and were often able to give information leading to the robbers' apprehension. In one noted case two horses stolen at Lutterworth were seen by the Leamington–Warwick coachman and he managed to bring the thief into Aylesbury for trial.

One Aylesbury coachman, Jem Wyatt, uncovered a murder and played his part in bringing the perpetrators to justice. One cold January morning in 1824 the *Despatch* left Aylesbury at its usual time of seven. The first turnpike gate was kept by 'a decent old fellow' called Needle. He customarily stood at the door, gate thrown open to let the coach through, but that morning was absent. Jem, surprised, got down to check that all was well. After repeated knocking he burst open the door. The old man's body lay on the floor, his head dreadfully beaten about, his wife across the bed, her head 'cruelly crushed' and 'equally bereft of life'.

Wyatt gave the alarm and carried the information along the road to London. Two suspicious 'gypsy-looking people', seen near the tollgate the previous night, were taken at Hemel Hempstead with the keeper's silver watch and four shillings hidden in their bloodstained clothes.[7]

News of less moment was daily carried by mail and stage. 'If a message had to be sent to any friend whose house it passed,' Llewellyn Jewitt recalled, 'it had only to be given *viva voce* or a slip handed up to ensure being duly and punctually delivered and a reply obtained.'

Coachmen and guards would bring requested items for people from neighbouring towns, throwing them off as they passed. They were equally adept at picking up. 'If it was a small packet or a note . . . [he] would take off his hat, hold it down at arm's length as the coach swept by while I . . . stretched up . . . and dropped it in, and cleverly it was done.'[8]

Some important missions were entrusted to coach crews. Ben Holmes drove past the Bracknell mansion of John Walter, proprietor of the *Times*. When staying there Walter would hand drafts for leaders and other instructions to Holmes, who had to rush the package to the newspaper office on arrival in London.[9] And it was common practice for country gentlemen to send important messages to London by coachman or guard. 'Many a time have they, as soon as they got to Fetter Lane, had to go to Crockford's Betting Club to back horses . . . on the eve of a race.'[10]

Farmers often sent rents to distant landlords. John Bayzand, coachman of the Oxford–Southampton *Oxonian*, for instance, collected the rents of the tenants of an Oxford college. And when the college president wished to see them it was by Bayzand they were summoned.

According to Bayzand's son, coachmen and guards were 'intelligent, pleasant, and as a general rule, civil, obliging, and always well dressed'. John 'would make his jokes, as he drove along, or say something quaint to his horses, and at all times endeavour to keep his passengers in merry mood . . . . He never would, if possible, let his passengers get down in the dumps; and I don't think they ever did.'

Miss Weeton, a Lancashire governess, on a trip from Liverpool to Manchester, 'had a very pleasant ride . . . for I soon got the seat by the coachman, who was very civil and communicative and described every object or place worth notice'.[11]

'These men were the "life of the road",' one enthusiast later recalled. 'The English coachman was almost invariably a hearty, cheerful fellow, full of anecdote, fond of chat, proud of his coach and . . . horses, and willing to impart information to travellers as to any object of interest . . ., was an artist in his craft, managed his high-mettled team with great skill and courage, was full of resource in case of accident, and was a sort of father to timid, nervous and young persons . . . placed under his care'.[12] Guards too were said to be 'full of romance and anecdote'.

They must have seemed knowledgeable and sophisticated to people who rarely travelled. Coachmen in particular came to be granted deference and respect. People vied with each other to sit next to them on the 'bench'. Their words seemed weighted with wisdom and were passed reverently from mouth to mouth.

Many were 'characters', a little eccentric in their ways, which all added to their image. Bob Hadley, who drove from Manchester to the Potteries, was full of fun, anecdotes and practical jokes, which made him a particular favourite. He wore a black or white hat with an outragiously broad brim, and a suit of extraordinary pattern, a large, eye-catching check.[13]

One guard, Benson, was an expert ventriloquist. His coach was once passed by a gig with a dog tied behind. Suddenly the air was filled with the most hideous sounds of a dog yapping and howling. The gig stopped, its occupants got down, but the dog was as right as rain. They remounted — with the same effect, until it was discovered the distraught dog was 'in fact' Benson.

Another time Benson rushed indignantly into an inn. Someone had put a pig in his coach boot. A group gathered round, giving advice on how to remove the animal, which could be heard screaming away inside. The guard then opened the boot to reveal to the astonished villagers that it contained only parcels.[14]

A guard of the Manchester–London *Telegraph*, Slugg remembered, was a tall, well-built, man named Pretty who always attracted much attention as the coach proceeded up

Market Street by his splendid bugle-playing. Many guards were masters of the keyed bugle, or sang to wile away the tedious hours for their passengers. Jack Goodwin, according to 'Old Roadster', was 'one of the most amusing guards on a coach I ever saw; full of anecdote and fun, he could imitate any animal on his key-bugle'.[15] They had wit and charm. McCluskie, a renowned guard on the Dublin and Boyle coach, was once reproached by two ladies for not playing 'The girl I left behind me' on his bugle, whereupon he replied, 'Why should I play it when all the pretty ones are with me?'[16]

Then there was the aesthetic angle. Most people 'made a stand' and watched the bright-coloured coach start off or go through, pulled by four fine horses. 'Next to a fox hunt,' wrote William Cobbett, 'the finest sight in England is a stage coach just ready to start ... [for] you see ... what man is capable of performing. The vehicle itself, the harness, all so complete and

'Most people "made a stand"' — at Reigate, on the road to Brighton

so neatly arranged; so strong, and clean and good; the beautiful horses, impatient to be off; the inside full and the outside covered, in every part, with men, women and children, boxes, bags, bundles; . . . the population and the property of a hamlet'.[17] And no matter how often 'the crack of th whip, the sound of the horn, or the rumble of the wheels was heard . . . about forty times a day did we raise our heads . . . to see them pass, and a pleasant sight it was'.

'There was no sameness in it,' Jewitt went on. 'Each time . . . there were new faces and new features to be seen, and each time there was the genial smile of the coachman, and the respectful raising of his whip, and the equally respectful recognition by the guard; and even the prancing horses seemed to put on extra freshness and extra vigour to be seen as they were driven gaily along . . .'

Then there was the adventure and the possibility of danger inherent in a long journey adding a certain excitement, especially on a dark, blustery winter evening — 'the spruce scarlet and gold liveries of the coachmen and guards coming out in bold relief with the fresh paint of the mails, whilst their lamps blazed away defying danger and darkness, and throwing a lurid glare upon the dull sludgy streets just then encrusted with a foretaste of the coming snowstorm'.[18] There was a 'feeling of serious reality about the whole thing, not unlike that which comes over one upon seeing a ship start on a long voyage or a regiment embarking for foreign service'.[19]

But what travellers most remembered in later life was the pleasure of sitting behind four well matched horses, exquisitely handled, stepping briskly along, to be changed 'like magic' at the next stage, 'the good-tempered smiling barmaid', the 'foaming tankard of real, sparkling, home-brewed beer', the guard's horn sounding 'Take your seats' and rolling on 'through a delightful country, the perfume from . . . fresh cut grass, or from a bean, pea, or clover field . . .'. Even night travelling (in summer) had 'a peculiar charm, a *je ne sais quoi* about it', wrote Stanley Harris. 'There was a something . . . most exhilarating in a gallop on a hard road on a moonlight night or at early dawn.'[20]

They remembered, too, the sumptious meals at inns which in turn were recalled with affection. James Hissey, wrote of 'that deservedly far and long-famed institution . . . the genuine old English coaching hostelrie. Before or since there has been nothing like to them.'[21]

Each had its specialities. At Oliver's Hotel, Bodmin, would be 'Cornish cream-potato pasties temptingly wrapped up in white paper, all got ready smoking hot . . .'. Similarly at little roadside 'publics'. 'The pride of one would be beer, another a home-made bacon, while a third might rejoice in a first-rate specimen of some locally manufactured cheese, pork pies, or sausages.' You went on your way 'rejoicing and refreshed'.[22]

In the relatively short period from 1815 to 1836 the stage-coach system underwent revolutionary changes and came to bear little resemblance to its lumbering eighteenth-century counterpart. When John Bayzand first drove the *Oxonian* the sixty miles from Oxford to Southampton in the late eighteenth century it involved twelve hours' hard slog. At the finish he

'A little roadside "public".' The Dorking coach approaching the Hand in Hand, near Box Hill, Surrey. *Julia Holmes*

was doing it smoothly in seven. On more important routes time-gains were even greater. Many factors contributed to these changes, which became general in the 1820s — better roads (McAdam had waved his magic wand), lighter and better designed coaches, improved harness, rapid changing of teams, shorter stops at inns and more skilled driving — but, above all, the principle which gave increasing rapidity was simple enough — horses were changed at ever more frequent intervals; every ten miles or so by the 1820s, compared with about twenty as many years before. Some stages were as short as six miles in the 1830s.

As the industrial revolution gathered pace, speed and efficiency improved, to meet growing demands for more rapid transit of passengers and light goods. The coaching industry grew dramatically. The average number of stagecoaches licensed in Britain in 1810–14 was 1,331 a year, growing to 3,036 in 1835, an increase of about 4·7 per cent a year. The most rapid growth probably came from 1823 after the post-war depression.[23] Millions of pounds came to the tied up in inns, coaches, horses (150,000 has been a commonly quoted figure), and about 30,000 is the general estimate of people directly employed — as proprietors, coachmen, guards, bookkeepers, clerks, porters, ostlers, innkeepers and their staffs. This may be a conservative estimate. As late as 1851 the census found 16,839 coachmen (not domestic servants), guards and postboys alone in Great Britain.[24] In addition there were the ancillary industries employing coachbuilders, harness-makers, whip and bugle makers, farriers, farmers and so on.

Coaching (and posting) brought quiet prosperity to many a humble village — like tiny Liphook in Hampshire where the Anchor Inn came to do a large business. The landlord employed fourteen servants and had three farms. Milk from ten cows was consumed daily, plus countries loaves from the baker, pork pies from the pie shop and viands from the butcher as refreshments for passengers on the twenty-six coaches and vans passing through every twenty-four hours.[25] It was the same in innumerable villages; and in coaching towns many tradesmen came to be dependent on the coaches. At Hounslow, the first stage out of London for western coaches, around 2,500 horses were stabled. Every one entailed £2 weekly outlay for maintenance. Thus a sum of £5,000 was circulated in the town each week, besides money spent by travellers at different inns.[26]

Coaching brought work where there had been none. New inns burgeoned across the country, usually converted from mansions, large houses and farmsteads. Often in isolated sites, but by the main road, they were extended to create a whole new area of industry in and around them. Opportunities appeared for many whose lot would have remained a great deal humbler, and, for some, coaches brought considerable wealth — to the great London coach proprietors like Chaplin, Horne, Sherman, Mountain, the Nelsons, Waterhouse, Fagg and Gray, but also to substantial proprietors in provincial towns and cities such as Costar in Oxford, Waddell in Birmingham, Lacey in Manchester, Brotherton in Liverpool, Outhwaite in Leeds, Teather in Carlisle, Piper in Edinburgh and so on.

In Ireland the impact of developments in passenger transport was probably even more revolutionary. The industry was dominated by one man — an Italian, Charles Bianconi. Most of Ireland came to be covered by his coaches and especially by his peculiar 'side-saddle' 'cars' (known affectionately as the 'Bians' after their owner). In 1815 public transport in Ireland was 'of a very limited character', confined chiefly to 'a few mail and day coaches running "few and far between"', and that only on the great lines of road, from some of the important cities to Dublin'. Along came the Italian, putting on his first car from Clonmel to Cahir in July 1815.

By 1843 he owned over a hundred vehicles, including mail coaches and different-size cars capable of carrying four to twenty passengers, travelling eight or nine miles an hour at an average fare of $1\frac{1}{4}d$ per mile. This was cheap and a dramatic boon to the poor, who had previously been unable to travel or had had to walk. His cars carried light goods too, causing a significant fall in prices.

In 1843 his vehicles were performing 3,800 miles daily, passing through over 140 'stations', each employing from one to eight 'grooms'. He owned around 1,300 horses consuming 3,000–4,000 tons of hay and 30,000–40,000 barrels of oats annually, purchased locally. Unlike most British proprietors, Bianconi built his own vehicles. In Clonmel, Sligo and Galway,

Bianconi's first car, later dubbed the 'faugh a ballagh' ('clear the way'). A larger version, holding five on each side and pulled by two horses, was nicknamed the 'Massey Dawson' after a popular Tory squire

the three depots of his organisation, there were car factories employing some twenty labourers plus skilled craftsmen. At its height the Bianconi establishment probably employed something over 600 men (and women) direct. And there were other coaching concerns — the Hartleys, the Bournes and John Talbot of Ballybrent among them.[27]

The coaching industry was an important economic force in itself but, above all, the system carried the country's commercial life-blood — shown only too dramatically when snow paralysed the network in 1836. Letters, bills of exchange, solicitors' papers, samples, large sums of money, commercial travellers, businessmen, dealers, tradesmen, farmers, were all whisked around the country in half the time taken before the French wars.

This rapid growth and improvement held the British in awe. They were proudest of all about their mail service, with its record of speed, punctuality and smartness, quickly established after Palmer's introduction of mail coaches in 1784. No other country could match its excellence, the British claimed. 'It was perfection.'

The speed and romance of coaching attracted younger elements among the 'upper ten thousand' — aristocrats and gentry — which further burnished its image. It was the excitement and art of driving four hourses at speed which first captured their interest, but driving their own carriages soon paled and they began, towards the end of the French wars, to lower themselves to travel by common stage and mail to pick up tips from 'real artists' and 'hold the ribbons'. Some became totally enamoured. 'The heirs to dukedoms, lords, baronets, and esquires, not only were driving their [own] four-in-hands, dressed as ... [public] servants, ... but they imitated their manners and conversation, and with their own private carriages mimicked the duty of the public ones, absolutely pulling up the White Horse Cellar and pretending to deliver parcels.'[28] Such people were only too happy to relieve coachmen of many hours' driving. Some even went so far as to become professional coachmen, driving a regular stint and pocketing tips

'It was perfection'

with the rest. All this gave a certain class to the coach industry and, equally, left these amateurs (and 'professionals') with pleasant 'childhood' memories.

For all these reasons the stagecoach came to hold a special place in the hearts of Englishmen, more so since they had barely grown used to it before it was gone. It was an affection which lingered on and lingers still — in Pollard prints, Christmas cards and coaching clubs. But, although it *may* have been the most perfect system of horse conveyance in the world, ever, it was not perfect enough for many.

2

A SERIOUS PENANCE

The British public had a love–hate relationship with the stage-coach, and the division was fairly clear cut — into those watching it pass and those forced to use it. There were notable exceptions in each camp, like other road users obliged to get out of the way — not always making it — as coaches galloped through. Conversely there were occasional travellers — to whom all was excitement — and enthusiasts who would brave any hardship to follow their passion beside the coachman behind a mettlesome four. The clergy often had a yen for coaching, like the Reverend Bird of Keswick, who, when he had not time to mount the box, would ride alongside the *Cuckoo* coach to see how the horses worked. The joke was 'the Cuckoo was *always* followed by a little bird'.[1] Another was the Reverend C. Atterbury of Christ Church College, Oxford, whose hobby it was to 'see the working of a well appointed coach and to sit behind a fine team skilfully handled'. For many years he spent his free time on coaches and would frequently go down the whole line to see 'all was right'. He was dubbed 'Costar's right-hand man'. On his last journey he wrangled long and hard with a fellow passenger for his usual seat of honour by the coachman. Finally succeeding, it became the seat of death. The coach was upset and the lamp iron pierced his skull.

John Spooner, coachman of the Gloucester mail between Henley and Oxford, drove the hearse, either from respect or because he did 'black' work on the side. Spooner drove so fast that he arrived at the church long before the procession. When the undertaker complained Spooner simply said, 'You couldn't drive fast enough for him when he was alive. I thought I'd give him a good shake-up when he was dead.'[2]

Atterbury never took the reins, but many gentlemen enthusiasts did (significantly adding to the accident rate) and it is their reminiscences that have given much of the romantic glow to the coaching age. Charles Dickens was tempted to join in the nostalgic euphoria in later life. He confessed to sometimes finding himself 'in common with some other people, affecting to lament' the passing of stagecoaches, but then memories of his many hard journeys flooded painfully back and he admitted that in reality 'everybody dreaded [them] as a serious penance then'.[3] Perhaps he leafed through his earlier writings. As a young reporter in the mid-1830s he wrote scathingly of 'all the tortures which the waiters, landlords, coachmen, guards, boots, chambermaids, and other familiars . . . might think proper to inflict'.[4]

Another frequent traveller, the editor of *Leisure Hour*, in recollecting 'Some Reminiscences of the Road' in 1874, was at pains to show that 'the dark side of stage coach travelling, even

'Those holes in Piccadilly called coach offices' — the White Horse Cellar (the 'last resource of human dejection'), 1821. *British Library*

in its palmiest times, was quite sufficient to overbalance all its fascinations'.

Travellers' difficulties, not to say humiliations, began at the coach office, usually a room set aside at an inn. They were not always a particularly edifying advertisement, especially in London — 'those holes in Piccadilly called coach offices' or 'ill-managed Piccadilly cellars' was one newspaper description.[5] Dickens was equally critical of the Golden Cross office at Charing Cross. 'Here,' he wrote after booking his ticket, 'a

'A mouldy-looking room'. The Golden Cross booking office. *Oxford University Press*

painful consciousness of your own unimportance first rushes on your mind.

'You enter a mouldy-looking room ornamented with large posting bills; the greater part of the place enclosed behind a huge lumbering rough counter, and fitted up with recesses that look like the dens of the smaller animals in a travelling menagerie without the bars. Some half dozen people are "booking" brown-paper parcels, which one of the clerks flings into the aforesaid recesses with an air of recklessness which you, remembering the new carpet-bag ..., feel considerably annoyed at; porters, looking like so many Atlases, keep rushing in and out, with large packages on their shoulders ...; one ... [clerk], with his pen behind his ear, and his hands behind him, is standing in front of the fire, like a full length portrait of Napoleon; the other, with his hat half off his head, enters the passengers' names in the books with a coolness which is inexpressibly provoking ....' Dickens went on to illustrate the misery of starting out from home at five-fifteen on a sleet-driven morning in anticipation of a long coach journey.

Porters seeing a traveller off did little to ease melancholy or anxiety. According to Tristram, the average London porter would be 'a ruffianly-looking fellow' breathing out brandy fumes as he demanded, 'What coach, your honour?' He would push his victim into the coach, fling the luggage into the boot, pocket his fee without so much as a thank you and then remorselessly attach himself to another innocent.[6]

Robert Eson, employed by Waterhouse at the Angel, Islington, did little to improve London porters' image as he attended the Birmingham *Eclipse*. As Eliza Semirot, a young Frenchwoman, was climbing the ladder the horses started momentarily forward. She fell and was fatally injured. John West, a passing grocer, reckoned the porter made no effort to catch or help her, but rather tried to prevent others from helping and was very abusive. Thomas Crowder, another onlooker, claimed that when he and others expressed sorrow Eson abused them in obnoxious language.[7]

Bookkeepers, too, could be curt. A respectable solicitor boarding the Exeter *Regulator* at the Swan with two Necks, in 1822, was appalled to see a vast quantity of luggage piled

'Climbing up the ladder'. *Julia Holmes*

illegally on the roof and, fearing an accident, complained to the
bookkeeper, who told him shortly and abusively it was
'no business of his or any one else what luggage was on the
roof'.[8]

The experiences of Miss Weeton, the Lancashire governess,
now aged forty-eight, on a London visit in May 1824, illustrate
some of the travails of the 'outside' traveller. Even in May it
was 'piercingly cold'. She had little time to eat and her life was
in 'imminent danger'. Nearing London, it began to rain, which
was *quite delightful!'* In another way she rather enjoyed the
novelty of journeying down through the night, peeping in at
'many an opened bedroom window' and 'many an object as I
passed along, aroused and interested'. But then, she was
experiencing a certain euphoria — 'since I left my husband [I]
have increased in bodily health and strength, so much as to be
better than I ever recollect'.

On the return journey the novelty wore thin. 'At the Inn [in
Birmingham] we changed coaches and took up six Irishmen of
the lowest description, which wholly destroyed the comfort of

the remaining part of the way, by their selfish rudeness. One
... had assumed my seat ... and I rode ... on a very dangerous
outside seat behind, backwards. We were four upon it, and it
was too short by much for this number; but every seat was
equally crowded. It was very necessary to keep my eyes open,
for the least drowsiness and I should have dropped headlong.
The man on my left kept a constant motion with his head upon
my shoulder up and down the night through, being heavy to
sleep, the brim of his hat endangering my eyes .... The iron
rail bruised me sadly, I was so jammed against it.'

At about six o'clock in the morning (she had started out from
Piccadilly before six the morning before!) one of the Irishmen
left his seat in front, and Miss Weeton was into it 'like a cat'.
She was more comfortable, 'although I had one on my left as
filthy as possible, and his head likewise jolting against me
perpetually. It was intolerable! I very quietly requested he
would let his head nod on the other ... side. I thought the
man would have beaten me. A young woman on my right, the
only female companion I had had, said she had passed a dreadful night, an Irish pig driver on each side of her, and another in
front, snoring and resting their heads against her, to prevent
themselves falling.'

Little wonder that passengers complained of being cramped.
William Bayzand, the *Mazeppa* guard, remembered the width
was, 'at a guess, five foot, six inches, for four people, little or
big. I always considered [it] very much too confined to be
anyways comfortable.' Even then he was over-generous in his
memory. Sixteen inches per person was the official allocation.
'Many [are] the times passengers have complained of their
small, cramped-up seat room allowed. My answer was, "That
is all the space Parliament has granted you."' A visiting
Frenchman in 1833 found the coaches' 'small size ... and the
short time they stop to refresh, render them very unpleasant
modes of conveyance'.[9]

For the four passengers inside there *was* more room, and
shelter from the elements, but one's fellow passengers could
be equally disagreeable. Lord William Pitt Lennox, a coaching
enthusiast, remembered it as 'not very pleasant to make one of
four, the other three consisting of a stout farmer, rude both in
health and manners, a fat nurse with a squalling child, and an

elderly invalid who insisted in having both windows up'. Another time there was 'a painted old Jezebel, redolent of Macassor oil and pachouli, a fledgling dandy strong of musk, a bloated publican on the verge of *delirium tremens*, who, as the old song says, "kept his spirits up by pouring spirits down"'. There was invariably a strong odour within. [10]

Sir George Head had to share the Buxton–Matlock coach with 'a fat married lady, holding a healthy little child on her lap with remarkably large staring eyes' who, to the discomfort of all, 'considered herself as if at home, and in her own nursery . . . making preparations that caused the whole party to look different ways'. [11] There were other drawbacks. On an earlier excursion from Manchester to Huddersfield, Miss Weeton recorded, 'The next morning was wet and I was obliged to travel inside . . ., in consequence of which I was very sickly . . ., and for two or three days after I got here was very unwell indeed'. The swaying motion of the coach affected many travellers.

Nor were Miss Weeton's fears of falling off unfounded. It was not uncommon for passengers to topple over the side. In October 1824 a passenger on the Banbury mail stood up to put his greatcoat on and, overbalancing, fell off and was killed. In September 1825 as the Inverness–Perth *Caledonian* approached Aviemore the guard got down to run alongside the horses, in case any stopped on the ascent. At the top he turned round to see a trunk, as he thought, fall off. It was in fact Andrew Swan, of the Commercial Bank of Edinburgh, who had fallen asleep and tumbled under the wheels. They got him into Aviemore, but in spite of bathing his feet in warm water, and his face, chest and hands in vinegar, he died murmuring, 'Oh! that I were in Edinburgh.' In 1837 one young man fell from the Leeds–Manchester *Umpire* when stationary. After passing through Delph passengers were alarmed by a frightened cry of 'Oh, my mother! my mother!' The coachman pulled up, to find a young lad lying by the hind wheel, his left leg wrenched off at the knee. He had been clinging to the coach for the ride, 'a very dangerous practice to which boys are much addicted'. The young man on top of the coach 'swooned away at the melancholy sight . . . and fell with great force from the vehicle, the front part of his head coming in contact with the ground. The blood gushed from him profusely.' [12]

There were more all-embracing accidents. The editor of *Leisure Hour* reckoned he could fill a whole sheet with details of calamities he had experienced. 'We have gone bodily, with a dozen companions, over a hedge into a bean field; we have burst through the crust of a gravel-pit . . . and been deposited in the ditch; we have come down with a crash on the stones through collision with a waggon, when a fellow passenger was killed on the spot; we have been left in the snow on a moonless night in consequence of the driver nodding on his box; and have come to grief in various ways, as well through weather or unavoidable accident, as by the neglect, the thoughtlessness, and the insobriety of those to whom the public safety was confided.'

Then there were the inns — those good old English inns travellers looked back on nostalgically. In reality they were rooked for every penny. Dickens's memories were not of 'the good–tempered smiling barmaid' but of the tap waiter at the Golden Cross. A quarter of an hour before the Birmingham *High-flier* was due to leave he requested a hot brandy-and-water. 'The first stroke of six peals from St Martin's church steeple just as you take the first sip of the boiling liquid. You find yourself at the booking office in two seconds, and the tap-waiter finds himself much comforted by your brandy-and-water, in about the same period.' In *Pickwick* he describes the travellers' room at the White Horse Cellar, Piccadilly, as 'the last resource of human dejection'.

The sumptious meals they remembered and paid for were rarely eaten in full because food often arrived deliberately late in the brief dinner stop, the intention being to use it again. 'You sat down,' recalled the editor, 'you carved the wing of a fowl for the lady opposite . . . were proceeding to help yourself when — lo! that is the coachman . . . crying "All ready!" and Mrs Nelson's confidential waiter is collecting the three-and-sixpence — and you have not taken a mouthful.' No one carved the fowl for Miss Weeton. Looking after Miss Stopford at the tea stop, she did not get 'half enough', so, at the breakfast stop, 'I took care this time to accommodate nobody, but let every-one look after themselves; for I have not found in this business that spirit of accommodation from others which I had a right to expect, but a very great deal of selfishness.' Thus the definition of a *true* gentleman was 'a gentleman at a stagecoach dinner'.

It was useless to 'expostulate and declare you have eaten nothing', the editor continued. Sometimes men would bear off viands to the coach 'to discuss them at leisure rather than be baulked of a meal for which they had paid the cash'. This had to be surreptitiously done, for the waiter would scurry after purloined provisions. One landlord pursuing a fowl spirited away in a handkerchief found the coach already on the move. Not to be outdone, he called out jeeringly, 'Won't you have the gravy, sir?' The other passengers had a good laugh at their humiliated companion.[13]

Two sailors on the Birmingham–London *Tantivy* were less easily intimidated, and when the guard blew his horn at the Star in Oxford they ran out brazenly with a loaf of bread and a fowl. The waiter followed to enquire what they were going to do with it.

'Eat it, mate.'

'But you're not allowed to take things away. Eat as much as you like and pocket none.'

'Then, mate, you should give us time,' they shouted back ferociously. 'We've got it, we've paid for it, mate, and we mean to eat it, mate!!!'

In the face of superior naval might the waiter slunk away.

Rarely were inns bested. The *Paul Pry* from Abergavenny stopped at the Star for supper, but poorer passengers would go to the near-by Bell, cheaper at sixpence each. A group of regular Welshmen saw no reason to pay when they ate and drank nothing.

'There,' protested Mrs Charlton, the landlady, after receiving sixpence, 'that's all I've received from the five, and they've been there for the twenty minutes before a good fire and gas.'

The following night eight Welshmen turned up. When the horn sounded, they rushed for the door, to find themselves prisoners.

'My demand is four shillings,' they were told. 'On the receipt of that sum I will open the door.'

An offer of 1s 6d 'for the three gentlemen that have had tea and coffee' followed another urgent blast.

'No matter, there was plenty for all. I shall not open the door till the 4s is paid.'

A final blow, and all the Welshmen, 'in a great funk in fear of being left behind', paid the money and ever after would all go in and have their sixpennyworth.[14] Perhaps the Welshmen were lucky to have had a good fire. Although the 'cheery blaze' often featured in nostalgic accounts, Dickens recalled that the poker was never among the irons lest travellers overstirred the miserly fire.[15]

No one was more disliked in the business than a tight traveller. John Fowler, son of the man who received news of Waterloo, wrote disparagingly of Camden Neild, a wealthy Chelsea barrister. 'He was of good family and a wretched miser .... I often remember him coming down, in the winter, sitting on ... Jem Wyatt's coach ... without a greatcoat or wrapper.' He had considerable landed property around Aylesbury, but never spent a shilling on his farms, exacting the utmost in rent. He was caught red-handed in a most heinous operation when lunching at the White Hart. 'On one occasion the waiter, coming unexpectedly into the room, found he had cut two large slices of bread, and had laid between them two thick slices of beef, and pocketed them, thus saving a dinner. He was charged an extra shilling for it, which he most reluctantly paid.'[16]

Nor was the quality of the meals always as remembered — 'with its scalding soup-stained warm water, its tough steaks, its Scotch collops, *"liquidis profusus odoribus"*, its underdone boiled leg of mutton, its potatoes, hot without and hard within'. In short, wrote Lord William Pitt Lennox, 'the dinners, with few exceptions, were execrable'.[17] 'English innkeepers', concluded Nimrod, 'are for the most part shamelessly indifferent to the comforts of coach passengers, and ought to be shown up oftener than they are.'[18]

Some travellers, to avoid the hurry and torture of sitting cramped days and nights at a time, broke their journey. Two gentlemen who dined and spent the night on the Dover road called for the bill and one overhead the landlord making it out.

'Please, sir, the gemmen in No. 5 wants their bill.'

'Very well,' said the landlord, 'let me hear what they had.'

'Soup, sir.'

'Soup, very well; what sort was it?'

'Mock turtle.'

'Mock turtle, 3s. Did they make any remark about it?'

'No, sir; only one of them said it was werry good.'

'Did they eat of it twice?'

'Yes, sir.'

'Oh, then, mock turtle, 5s; now go on.'

'Fried sole and shrimp sauce.'

'Fried sole 2s; shrimp sauce 1s—3s. Did they make any remark about that?'

'One o' them said that the fish was werry fresh.'

'Indeed! Then fried sole 3s, shrimp sauce 1s 6d—4s 6d. Now go on.'

'Small leg of Welsh mutton, potatoes and French beans.'

'Mutton 5s; potatoes 1s; French beans 5s; rather early for French beans, isn't it?'

'Yes, sir; both the gemmen remarked that it was werry early.'

'Oh, then, French beans 10s.'[19]

Nor was the accommodation always as salubrious as one might expect. Two well known coaching inns in Holborn, the George and Blue Boar and the Bell and Crown, had their rooms over the stables and were consequently 'full of fleas and bugs'.[20] Dickens has David Copperfield finding the Golden Cross 'a mouldy sort of establishment', while his bedroom 'smelt like a hackney coach and was shut up like a family vault'. But the great writer reserved his greatest contempt for another. 'Never were there such labyrinthine uncarpeted passages, such huge numbers of small dens for eating and sleeping in, beneath any one roof as are collected together beneath the "Great White House" at Ipswich.' Other attractions were '. . . a dying fire in a dirty grate, an hour's wait for a meal, and a waiter with a fortnight old napkin'.[21]

So much for the 'insolent extortions of . . . purveyors of refreshments on the road'.[22]

3

LOW FELLOWS

The *Railway Times* also fairly drew attention to 'fees to drivers, guards, porters, and the thousand-and-one extortioners who, under the old system, made travellers their lawful prey — not only robbing, but insulting them also'. For woe betide the passenger who neglected to cough up the necessary. It was rare that they went as far as John Spencer, driver of a Manchester coach, who struck his fare, Alice Wray, when she refused to tip him. That was in 1847 when coaching was almost extinct, tempers were short and neurosis the order of the day. There were more subtle means, brought to perfection since the earliest coachman had scathingly complained of his tip as 'a groat of more than ordinary thinness'.[1] Few passengers had the strength of character to withstand a coachman's sarcasm. Throwing a meagre tip away was another gesture calculated to embarrass, but there were always some hardened regulars. The coaching industry got them in the end. James Wood, a wealthy Gloucester banker, was always niggardly, but John Spooner finally got his own back. When Spooner asked for his fee at Henley two gentlemen gave him a shilling each but 'Jimmy' Wood gave, as he thought, sixpence. Spooner jerked his arm as if throwing it away in disgust. Wood immediately discovered he had given half-a-sovereign by mistake and demanded its return.

'Well, you saw what I did with it,' replied Old John smugly, 'and by this time I should think it's at the bottom of the Thames.'

'I shall write to Mr Costar, your proprietor,' retorted the banker.

'I should think you never was such a silly ass as to throw it away,' Costar later said after reproaching him.

'No, sir,' was the reply, 'it fell in my little side-pocket, and I did the miserable, niggardly banker.'[2]

One Cambridge doctor of divinity refused to tip Richard 'Hell-fire Dick' Vaughan after a bout of foul language. Apologies proved unavailing.

'My carpet bag is in the front boot and that large trunk on the roof is mine.'

'Here's your carpet-bag, your reverence. As you've done your duty I must do mine. I'll take that trunk to the office and have it weighed. And I think your reverence will have seven and sixpence to pay for it.'[3]

As one foreign visitor concluded, 'The taste for travelling, an expensive taste in any country, is truly a ruinous one in England,' and although it might, in some ways, be more pleasant than in other countries 'one is steeled against this seductive consolation by the perpetual warning of a speedily drained purse'.[4] A journey from London to Edinburgh, for example, cost about £14 inside and £10 outside with the inevitable 'extras'.

Further, the little missions so cheerfully undertaken merited reward, and coachmen often had an exaggerated sense of their worth. John Adams, who drove the Oxford–London *Defiance* was presented with some fresh-cut greens at Dorchester — the gift of a farmer he had done some small service.

'Oh, is that all Mr D. sent?' asked Adams arrogantly.

'Yes, sir.'

'Take them back and tell your master the greens are of no kind of use to me without one of your fat barn-door fowls, or a piece of home-cured bacon.'

Next morning two large bundles of greens, a splendid fowl and a piece of bacon arrived. 'Tell Mr D. that's more like business, and Mr Adams is very much obliged to him; and here's a shilling for your trouble.'

The countryman looked thoroughly pleased, pulled his billy-cock two or three times, and thanked the coachman, bidding him 'Good morning, sir.'[5]

Many coachmen (and guards) did get carried away by their own importance — especially when the aristocracy began to ape and fawn on them. Later reminiscences built them into nobler creatures than they often were. Some were downright rogues. Tom Hennesy, coachman of the Stamford–London *Old Regent* was glorified in Reynardson's *Down the Road*, but a reviewer cautioned what 'a shocking blackguard' he really was.[6] Accounts by non-enthusiasts were usually more direct. George Borrow claimed in *Romany Rye* they 'considered themselves mighty fine gentry, nay, I verily believe the most important personages of the realm'. They were in fact 'low fellows' but masters at driving when driving was in fashion.

Grantley Berkeley never felt inclined to 'become the bosom friend of the driver . . . simply because he drove a four-horse coach, winked at the pretty barmaids . . . , wore a low-crowned broad-brimmed hat . . . '. He reckoned that the 'class whence these coachmen came was not one famed for its position or education', and most 'respectability' agreed. When Parson Bird took over the Whitehaven–Lancaster coach, the regular driver having broken his leg, he dropped off a lady at the Turk's Head, Kendal. A ball was being held in the town that evening, and Bird asked her to dance. She indignantly refused — 'she was come of a good family and had more respect for herself than to dance with a coach driver' (although within the year she had become Mrs Bird).[7]

Most saw the coaching craze as silly. Grantley Berkeley, who would never normally have dreamt of travelling by stage, was persuaded by Harry Wombwell to go down to Newbury. They had the back seat to themselves. 'Instead of sitting by my side as easy as he could make himself, and like a gentleman, Harry sat in a sort of one-side position, both hands stuffed into his greatcoat pockets, and his hip resting on the rail or arm of the seat.'

'Why the deuce, Harry!' exclaimed Berkeley, after regarding him for a time with some curiosity, 'do you sit in that agonised way, like a cock on a too narrow perch? Here's lots of room for you!'

'Beg pardon, sir,' he replied, throwing up a first finger to his hat, 'but it's my pleasure to make the passengers as comfortable as I can. If you've room enough, sir, I'm satisfied.'

'Don't be such an infernal ass!' retorted Berkeley. 'You're not the guard.'

'As you please, sir,' again throwing a finger to his hat.[8]

The so-called 'gentleman coachman' was in fact, according to Berkeley, 'a decayed gentleman, or a young man whose extravagance had outrun the constable, or who was addicted to low company'. This was certainly true of the first gentleman coachman, Bobart, who had been at an Oxford college hence dubbed the 'Classical Coachman'. He drove on the Oxford road and corrupted such freshmen as he was able. Son of an Oxford college principal, he was brought to 'degradation by a passion for gaming and driving, which had usurped every just and moral feeling. His father felt his conduct deeply . . . His miserable mother having advanced him all her remaining property; was now reduced to a dependance upon the benevolence of a few liberal-minded Oxford friends, and this son was now so lost to every sense of shame that he *preferred* the Oxford road to exhibit himself on in his new character of a university whip.'[9] 'Gentleman Dean, driving in the West Country, was a later, less debauched, version of the same species, having fallen victim to the 'exorbitant bills and extortionate usury' of Oxford tradesmen.[10]

In 1830 one missionary organisation found it 'evident that coachmen, guards, hackney coachmen, chaise drivers, porters, waiters, ostlers, boots, and stable boys at inns live in a systematical source of iniquity and wickedness'. Coachmen in particular were reputed to be great ones with the girls.

Guards were perhaps more aware of their position in contacts with the fair sex. When Blake, a drunken guard of the London–Devonport *Quicksilver* mail, fell from grace in 1832 Maria Besley, whose father kept the inn at Newton Bushel, reckoned, 'His manners were different to what I had before seen them. They were anything but respectful. He spoke in a more familiar manner than guards usually do.' Still, honour was maintained. 'He didn't take any liberty with me,' she asserted, perhaps with a note of regret.[11] But there was another Quicksilver man, Tommy Walters — a 'notorious little guard' — who got left behind in Newton Abbot, because, he admitted, 'I was kissing the pretty girl in the post office!'[12]

Working with stagecoaches did something for a man. When Charles Fashnact, an assistant porter at the Swan with two Necks, was suspected of stealing a parcel he was searched,

'Your genuine coachman is invariably a ladies' man'

revealing two letters from discarded mistresses, the first addressed to his current fancy, Miss Humphreys.

'Miss, — I am astonished to think as you should keep company with such a low lad as Charles, for when he first spoke to me he behaved very well, but when he completed *is* desire he used me very ill. I have got over my confinement. I hope I shall be no more trouble to him. I take this liberty of writing this epistle to you, hoping it will be a warning to you, as he has seduced two young girls. Ann Lushington.'

'Dear Charles — This comes with my kind love to you to no wher I have offended you that you did not speak to me larst night. I did not no that I had. If I have, let me now. You seame to say that I care nothing about you, but if I did not I should not took the troble to wark till nine o'clock last night. Pleas to send it anser as sun as you can. By doing you will mutch oblige. Yours, E. Gisbourne.'

Charles Fashnact was fourteen years old and stood 4 ft 6 in. in his boots![13]

As for horse keepers and stable men, they were, according to John Chaplin, a retired coach proprietor, in 1831, 'men of a class whose morals I cannot say a great deal in favour of'. Peter Mountain reckoned, 'some of them are a bad set; they are men of no education, and neither can read nor write'.[14] In Ireland, Charles Bianconi found it difficult to get 'men who are sober and sufficiently intelligent and honest for such important trust as is reposed in them'.[17]

Passions sometimes ran deep in stables too. All was quiet at the Bear Inn, Wantage, early one morning. Suddenly Lamball, the ostler, awoke and found Poole, the stable hand, about to stab him in the throat with a large carving knife. Lamball grappled with him and succeeded in getting the weapon, but received a dangerous wound in the stomach. 'The cause of the rash act is supposed to be jealousy, as it seems that Poole had formed an attachment for one of the female servants, which was not encouraged on her part, and he imagined that Lamball was preferred before him.' Ostlers were frequently in trouble.[16]

Possibly, too, the cheerful chatter of coachman and guard, their eccentricities and practical jokes, could become wearying to regular travellers, and certainly to the butts of their humour. One of Bob Hadley's little games when guard was to take bets that he could make any pedlar he saw drop his pack. Coming across a Scots draper trudging along, Hadley would wait until well past, then shout to the man and point some way behind him. Invariably the man dropped his pack and ran back, leaving the guard collecting his winnings, the passengers highly amused. Jack Goodwin — 'the finest performer on the keyed-bugle the ''road'' ever knew' — once imitated a donkey's bray when two old women were driving a donkey. It bolted and galloped alongside for more than a mile, to the passengers' delight. The opinions of Scottish drapers or old women with donkeys are not recorded.[17] The views of one duped Irishman are. William Motrham, a Yorkshire guard with an inexhaustible fund of humour, used to amuse passengers with racy anecdotes. He told a plausible story as to why Chesterfield church spire was crooked. The Irishman listened with interest how it was to be straightened and moved on rollers next day. 'Begorry, thin, oi'll just stop and see it done!' He was put down, but soon discovered he had been hoaxed, and there stood 'a wild Irishman swearing eternal vengeance on all coach guards'.[18]

In truth many crews were 'civil and obliging' to those to whom it paid to be. George Borrow wrote of acts 'of brutality practised upon the weak and unoffending — upon some poor friendless woman travelling with but little money, and perhaps a brace of hungry children with her or upon some thin and half-starved man travelling . . . from London to Liverpool, with only eighteenpence in his pocket after his fare was paid, to defray his expenses on the road . . . but when nothing was given . . . — and nobody was bound to give them anything . . . — then what a scene would ensue!'

A Post Office inspector wrote despairingly that half his time was employed in dealing with letters of complaint from passengers about the 'improper conduct and language of guards'. One passenger complained of being drenched by water coming through the roof. The only answer he got was 'Ay, mony a ane has complained o' that hole,' and the guard quietly passed on to other duties.[19]

Then one might get with one of Fagg's guards on the Dover coach. Stanley Harris got up with him to have a chat. 'I found him, however, so unsociable and so unapproachable, that . . . I returned to my seat on the box and on communicating to the coachman the futile efforts I had made, he said, "Yes, sir, he is a very separate man." '[20]

Or a passenger might get with short-tempered John Spooner. One wrote to Costar complaining of Spooner's incivility and got him suspended. Eventually reinstated, Mr Costar told him: 'and take my advice, keep your tongue still'.

The first night, a gentleman on the box asked Spooner several questions. He kept quiet; so the gentleman asked the guad, 'Is our coachman deaf?'

'A little, sir.'

Later: 'Coachman, whose residence that?'

No answer. Repeated much louder. Finally Spooner announced in a great rage and very loud, 'It's not mine or yours, or you wouldn't ask such foolish questions. Perhaps you'll try and say I'm not civil.'[21]

Regular travellers had many tales to tell of how they were ill used; complaints featured in the contemporary press were glossed over in later accounts. It was not unusual for passengers to have to pay more at the end of the journey than had been agreed at the beginning, and this money was often collected most arbitrarily. Thomas Shorelan, an Irish journeyman carpenter, arriving at Liverpool in 1824, took the *Royal Umpire* 'with a clear bargain, that on his paying £2 2s, nothing more would be required . . .' on arrival in London. Two days later he was surprised by a visit from William Duff, book-keeper at the Saracen's Head, with the *Umpire's* guard, demanding an extra 16s for conveyance of his luggage and on his refusing to pay they made off with a great coat and clothes' box. It was another clear instance of the 'arbitrary conduct of stage coach proprietors, in taking the law into their own hands', thundered the *Times* on 2 April 1824, but it continued to occur. In 1834 Mr Marrilier paid his fare in Bristol but in London had his luggage, worth £50, impounded at the Blossoms unless he paid another 15s for a babe-in-arms, legally entitled to travel free.[22]

Even worse, Nicholas Whitworth, a corn dealer, had a dreadful time at the hands of Stringer, guard of a North Wales mail. 'On the 21st of September last [1826],' he related, 'I took a place . . . at Bangor and paid for it. When I got to Holyhead I . . . was walking down to the packet . . . [when] Stringer . . . came to me: he said I had not paid my fare . . . . I said I had paid my fare at Bangor and had seen my name and the money entered in the waybill. He said that would not do for him; I had not paid, and must pay. I refused, and he laid hold of me and dragged me towards Spencer's Inn [the Eagle and Child]. ''By G–d I'll lay you £5 that you haven't paid your fare, nor is your

name in the waybill.''
I said, "Done."' '
A gentleman agreed to hold the money. Stringer then pulled out the bill. The name and money paid, 6s, were clearly marked and Whitworth took up the money.
But Stringer demanded his £5 back.
'I have no £5 of yours. I have £5 that I won from you and I shall keep that,' retorted Mr Whitworth.
'He then laid hold of me, and dashed me against the wall. I went out . . ., he followed, threatening me, saying I should not go out of Holyhead till I had given him the £5 back: he kept dashing me against the wall.'
Whitworth sought shelter in the travellers' room, then stepped out cautiously to head for the packet, but Stringer pounced once more and 'in a great rage laid hold of me again; he swore I should never go on board the King's packet till I had given him back the £5 and paid my coach fare . . ., he began to shake me violently, and I bawled out murder, as I was afraid of him; he said . . . he would shoot me . . ., ran to the coach and brought his firearms from it . . . came towards me and presented one at me'.
Fortunately a woman came running and turned his arm, shouting, 'For God's sake, man, what are you going to do?' and Whitworth was able to escape into the Eagle and Child again. Mrs Spencer now appeared on the scene, aroused by the disturbance, but rather than pitying Whitworth she ordered him out. 'I said, that's impossible, would you have me go out into the street to be murdered by that villain?' She still ordered him out, refused him a bed (by this time he had missed the packet) and finally sent for the constable — to arrest not Stringer but Whitworth.
The constable, determined to do his duty by Mrs Spencer — 'I suppose if Mrs Spencer ordered you to shoot me, you'd do it,' Whitworth cried tartly — flashed his truncheon and his handcuffs, and laid hold of the unlucky dealer, whose 'blood began to boil'. Then in walked Stringer. 'I appealed to . . . [them] to protect me from his violence. Stringer paid no attention, but came up to me, and in rather civil terms begged I would give him the £5 back . . . and I gave it him, as he said it would ruin him if I did not.'

Stringer was later punished by the Sessions, but the harassed traveller lost the case for assault and false imprisonment against Mrs Spencer and the constable.[23]

Stringer's actions seem quite unaccountable. Could it be that he was 'so so'?

4

HALF-SEAS-OVER

Alas, porters were not alone in breathing out brandy fumes. Alcohol oiled the wheels a good deal. Ostlers were well known for drunkenness, and, worse, crews often drank more than was good for them — or for their passengers, who in turn were often well topped up to anaesthetise them from the journey's discomforts. Staid Miss Weeton's life was in 'imminent danger' not only from her precarious position but, she admitted, 'on account of the drowsiness occasioned by the brandy and water I took'. One passenger from Brighton got so drunk that he laid himself down on the roof, but soon began to roll about and finally rolled off. Luckily other passengers managed to grasp his cloak so that he hung 'like a spread eagle' until let down and pushed inside.[1]

Even a top guard was not immune. Admittedly Blake, guard to the crack *Quicksilver*, was not on duty himself but on his way from Exeter to Devonport on the Bath mail on 2 May 1830. At first he sat with coachman, James Corder, but soon went inside, where Mrs Pilfold was on her way to join her husband, a half-pay naval captain.

Blake was 'in a high state of drunkenness, and . . . soon became painfully disgusting, as the dose he had taken created nausea which with difficulty he suppressed, and which caused his unhappy companion to move as far from him as possible'. The guard took offence and let fly with 'a torrent of abuse, oaths and execrations too gross for the worst description of female to repeat, wanting to know from what rat-hole she came, and frequently using the epithet "bitch", and such like lauguage'. Poor Mrs Pilfold was quite 'set back' and 'knocked up' by it all, and 'laboured under great excitement and delirium for some days', according to Cornelius Tripe, Devonport surgeon.

Evidence from witnesses along the route made it clear that Blake, Corder and amorous Thomas Walters, the guard on duty — twenty-five years a mail guard — had over-indulged. George Slyfield, innkeeper at Armbridge, reckoned 'they appeared in such a state that I thought it prudent not to notice the circumstance. They appeared to me to have been drinking, and to have had enough. Blake appeared to be half seas over.'[2]

It is only justice to point out that drunkenness was not a problem confined to coaching, and coach people were probably no worse than contemporaries, with the exception that since the industry was so centred on inns they were perhaps exposed to greater temptation, opportunity and, possibly, had more funds to indulge the pastime. There was probably much free liquor available too. Equally it is easy to understand how the 'circumstances of stage coachmen, their midnight travelling, their exposure to all weathers, would ... require the use of strong fermented liquors to "keep out the cold", "the wet", "the fog" and "keep the wind off their stomachs"'.[3] Since coaching was such a public business, inebriation was the more obvious.

Hyde reckoned Post Office guards were 'given to take drink ... too often', and when Jack Brett, guard to the Devonport–Bristol *Nonpareil*, turned a back somersault and injured his head 'alcoholic fever' was said to be the cause, but, to be fair, reported instances of guards being drunk, on or off duty, are rare.[4] Mail guard Moses Nobbs took his father's advice never to 'damage his own health by drinking other people's' and most guards seem to have seen of the same stamp. Even if they did take a glass, the consequences were less hazardous than when drivers drank, as they more often did. In 1827 Mr Peacock, solicitor to the Post Office, reckoned that 'it was too much the habit of coachmen to drink upon the road, which was the principal cause of the many accidents that occurred'. Austin, driver of a westbound coach in 1823, was so 'beastly drunk' that when trying to get off the box after scraping a waggon he fell head-first between the horses. The passengers refused to go another yard with him despite the remoteness of the spot and early morning hour. The guard — 'whose steadiness and good conduct deserve great praise' — was obliged to take the reins and bring the coach safely into Salisbury, the coachman lolling behind.

Another guard saved the day in November 1827 when George Morley, 'totally incapable of driving', wrapped up the Bristol mail near Hounslow, in spite of the guard's repeated cautions to which he 'appeared not to pay any attention'. Guard and passengers patched up the mess and he drove safely on to Newbury.[5]

Edward Jenkins, 'who was intoxicated at the time', drove the London mail over a 121 ft precipice near Llandovery on 19 December 1835 despite the passengers' entreaties, and Thomas Crouch drove the London–Lincoln up mail into the down mail near Biggleswade in 1837 'owing to a sudden curvature in the road and the wandering of his faculties'.[6] It was the death of Crouch, and many travellers died and were injured for the same reason.

Quite often, like Crouch, coachmen suffered most from their foolishness. Moses Nobbs remembered how once, on leaving Picadilly, his coachman was unfit to drive, so he strapped him in the guard's seat and took over as far as Whitchurch. There the coachman insisted on driving, but a jolt threw him between the horses and under the wheels, killing him instantly.[7] Thomas Cross once 'over-stepped the bounds of prudence' and although determined to be 'doubly particular and careful' met the Manchester *Cobourg* on a turn near Mimms at sixteen miles an hour: 'my leaders flew out of the road . . . over a small ditch on to a bank . . . but the sudden jerk . . . threw me off, and I lay on my back in the road, and, for a moment, saw the coach falling on me; but . . . the body of the coach struck . . . [a] post . . . and righted . . . — a most miraculous escape for me'.

Cross learned his lesson and resolved never to drink and drive again. 'I assure my readers that, in my long career, it was never repeated.' Others were less sensible.[8] Some coachmen were virtually alcoholics — but continued to drive. Tom Bradley remembered how it 'was a treat to see a crowd of pigmy postboys turn out to hoist a . . . driver of the *Wellington* [London–Newcastle] into the box seat. He was a very stout

'I . . . saw the coach falling on me.' Thomas Cross learns his lesson.
British Library

man, and mostly half-seas-over, and it was impossible for him to reach that eminence without help, but he treated the lads well, and they always turned out to give him a lift. He generally promised them half-a-gallon . . . , and he used to say during the operation . . . : ''Altogether, another push up, lads, an' I'll mak it a gallon!'' ' William Bramley, who drove the *Rockingham* north of Leeds, 'was always more or less drunk', and there were many like him until the end of coaching.

Some remained remarkably laconic about the business. One whose intoxication had spread sixteen passengers over the countryside from the Fakenham at 1.00 a.m. was found lying in a ditch at six o'clock by a doctor, who asked whether he was hurt. He replied no, and he hoped nobody else was, but when asked to get up said he would get up when he pleased.[9]

Other coachmen were not obviously drunk but, their senses impaired, were ill equipped to meet the emergencies which were part and parcel of coaching life, and this frequently resulted in smashes. Miss Weeton set out with great pessimism in 1824 — 'ere another sun sets, these eyes may have been closed for ever; ere another day dawns these limbs may have become stiff and cold . . . ' — and with fatalism, 'but oh, if I am but with Thee, Thou Great and Mighty Un-nameable, what need I care'. In this state of mind she set off for London, 'considering it to be very probable that I should never reach it; when such numbers are killed by the overturning of coaches, what right have I to expect to escape?'

Coach travel was indeed fraught with hazard and, in terms of passenger miles, probably had a higher death and injury rate in this period than any previous or subsequent form of public transport by land. True, the numbers travelling by coach were relatively small, and in any accident it was rare for more than one or two to be killed. Obviously consequences of, say, a crowded train crashing at speed were far more calamitous than a coach upset.

The fact remains that official returns show twenty people killed and seventeen injured by railways (only ten of the dead were actual passengers) out of 44 million who travelled over those lines 1830–38.[10] The number of coach passengers must have been less, but the numbers killed and injured were much higher. Newspapers are studded with details of accidents where people died or were gravely injured.

The accident rate was high partly because of the nature of the animal. The coach, pulled by four fickle beasts, was high off the ground and prone to overset at the least provocation from such trifles as a small pile of stones, or simply when excess speeds got it 'on the rock' so the slightest undulation or deviation would sent the whole lot over. In Ireland accidents were few, since the cars were of safer design. As Bianconi explained, 'The construction . . . renders it impossible to upset, for the whole weight is outside the wheels . . . consequently the passengers on the one side answer as a counterpoise to the passengers on the other'. In twenty-three years as a car owner he had never had one upset. Even if they ran into a bank the front-wheels were so low that the axles merely embedded themselves into it.[11]

The results to the higher, more stylish British coach were also more catastrophic if any part broke down — accidents caused by an axle breaking, a pole splintering, a wheel coming off or a piece of harness snapping were legion, but generally the human element was involved, through overloading, faulty maintenance or carelessness.

'The whole weight is outside the wheels.' The *Finn McCoul*,
Bianconi's largest car, named after Ossian's Giant

Accidents from breakdowns did not occur 'so much as they
used to' William Chaplin told an inquiry in 1835, 'because the
roads are so much better and smoother that there is not so
much obstruction as there used to be'. Coaches were also
better built and maintained, but breakdowns continued to be
an important source of accidents.[12]

Many accidents were due simply to 'driver error'. If their
faculties were not impaired by drink coachmen were careless
incompetent or simply cussed.

From this distance in time, accidents take on an unreal
quality and visions of people flying over hedges to land in
manure heaps or gorse bushes raise more of a smile than a tear
— like the Keystone Cops. There was, for instance, the woman
outside on the Duke of Lancaster, flung neatly on to a high
hedge, where she was found perched with no injury but a few
scratches from the thorns, 'and a vehement palpitation from
the alarm'.[13]

One mail guard in Scotland was thrown off and temporarily
stunned. Coming to, he imagined something wrong with his
head. He felt a flat surface which, he was convinced in his
mazy state, was a section of his neck, his head having been cut
off. It was in fact the crown of his hat, which had been forced
down over his face.[14]

Then there is the picture conjured up of the *Royal Fleece*
starting out from Huddersfield in 1823 laden with Methodist

'If any part broke down'. *British Library Newspaper Library*

preachers on their way to the annual conference at Sheffield. Going down Shelley Bank, Edmund Smith drove his horses to full speed with wheels unlocked, observing, 'if he couldn't make them run up the hills he'd make them run down'. The coach gathered momentum, came to a curve and overturned with a tremendous crash, causing a significant number of the West Riding Circuit to fly in diverse directions before descending to earth.

In films, of course, victims get up and walk away, if not on the screen then off it — but the Reverends Sargent and Lloyd did not. They died, and others were injured.[15]

There was nothing particularly amusing about the scene of an accident — passengers dazed and moaning in and around the smashed coach; horses stricken and frightened. Peter Smith, a watchmaker, saw the London–Liverpool *Standard* go over in Coventry in 1830, with ten passengers aboard. It was half-past midnight and 'when it turned the corner, there seemed a great confusion amongst the horses . . .; the fire that struck from the horses' feet was like a flash of lightning and instantly the coach fell over'. He saw the guard staggering up behind the coach, 'the side of his face was all over blood'. An inside passenger was muttering, 'Bad management! Bad management!'

'A significant number of the West Riding Circuit'. *Banbury Guardian*

John Gutteridge, another watchmaker, also rushed to the scene and helped the coachman, Thomas Platt, up. 'I think he was in a state of intoxication; he smelled very strong of liquor, and was very unsteady . . .; he was sick . . . I saw him heaving, I can't say that he vomitted; . . . he said he was hurt and groaned.'

He turned his attention to William Cooper, now visible by the light of a candle brought by Reverend Grindon. He was lying with a heavy white box on his head, weltering in blood pouring from his ear. Gutteridge took the box off. 'I picked him up in my arms, and brought him into Mr Grindon's house,' where he died soon afterwards.[16]

Another unpleasant spectacle followed the *North Star's* crash near Preston in 1827. The coach was dragged a few yards after it fell, and a young servant girl's leg, trapped under the iron railing, was 'lacerated in a dreadful manner'. The limb was amputated but she died shortly afterwards. Her mistress, Mrs Clayton, broke her collarbone and 'was not likely to recover'. A child inside was seriously hurt. Ball, the driver, had a thigh, leg and arm broken and one eye knocked out. A verdict of manslaughter was later returned against him: he was said to have been driving at a 'most furious rate', but he was 'beyond mortal account.'[17]

Almost as bad as the accident itself was the realisation that a crash was imminent and there was nothing for it but sit tight and wait for the inevitable. In November 1827 the *True Blue* Leeds–Wakefield upset. Stagecoaches did not have brakes. To slow them down hills, a metal skid pan ('skid', 'slipper' or 'shoe') was slipped under a rear wheel to lock it. Coachman William Herfield, decided to press on without skid down Belle Hill.

At first the horses proceeded quietly but then, feeling the increasing weight, gatherered momentum until they over-mastered Herfield and were galloping flat out. The coach began to rock and sway ominously. William Lee, a Leeds spirit merchant, grimly expressed fears to the other insides that they were about to have an accident. Mrs Wood, on top, went further and screamed, 'Oh! coachman, stop! You're killing us all.'

All might yet have been well, since the road ran straight from the bottom of the hill, was clear for fifty yards, and there were only two stationary carts ahead. There was room to pull up before, and plenty of room to pass. But the horses were beyond stopping. Herfield's 'self-possession' was 'paralysed' and they were heading dangerously near the carts.

Sarah Smith, a collier's wife, standing outside her cottage opposite the carts watched horror-struck as the coach thundered closer.

'Stop, coachman; stop; stop! You'll be killing all the ladies and gentlemen.'

Herfield was aroused sufficiently to give the horses a 'flog', but not in the right place. They turned into the carts rather than away.

The coach wheel locked with a cart wheel, throwing the cart on its side, and Herfield off the coach, which went on several yards before overturning, horses' feet and wheels striking 'fire like lightning' in the darkness.

Mr Lee scrambled out unscathed, but found the coachman 'quite dead'. He lifted him up and blood ran out of his head, ears, nose and mouth 'most profusely'. The outsides had, as always, come off worst. James Burrell, a Knaresborough overseer, was crying out from beneath the coach, the full weight on his thigh. His leg was later amputated but he died in

the night. Charles Cope, a Leeds artist and drawing master —
'a gentleman universally and deservedly respected' — also died
later.[18]

Lost in time, these long-dead victims hardly tear at our heart-
strings, but then, as now with our road accidents, each
represented a small area of grief and tragedy. Accident accounts
— 'he left a widow pregnant and four helpless children to
deplore the loss of an indulgent husband and affectionate
father' or 'left without means of support' — indicate the
unhappiness caused by a moment of carelessness.

Imagine too the anguish of Mr Brodrick, a Macclesfield man,
whose eighteen-year-old son — 'a young man of great promise
and most estimable qualities' — had gained a public exhibition
at Brasenose College, Oxford. Mr Brodrick, after a trip to
London, returned via Oxford to visit his son, coming up to
university by the *Regulator*. Loaded to an 'enormous and
unusual height, in consequence of the great rush of members
into the University at the commencement of term', on making
a sharp turn near Banbury the coach went over and young
Brodrick was thrown off and killed. Mr Brodrick was waiting
at the terminal inn when a messenger mentioned casually the
coach had been upset and his son killed.[19]

Mrs Wood injured her arm badly in the *True Blue* accident
and, although we hear no more of the poor lady, no doubt for
her the matter did not end there. In the days of primitive
medicine such fractures, dislocations and contusions as
newspapers briefly reported meant weeks of suffering and
considerable expense. Mr Williams, injured when the Oldham–
Leeds *True Briton* overturned in 1824, sustained bruises
which 'made him lame for thirteen or fourteen weeks and
prevented him from carrying on his business, by which he
had been in the habit of gaining from thirty to forty shillings a
week'.[20] Mr Chambers, a Leeds clerk, was injured in an upset
of the mail near Huddersfield. He was 'taken up quite insen-
sible, and conveyed to a neighbouring public house. A surgeon
was sent for, who . . . found him in a very weak state and
exceedingly sick. One of his shoulders was dislocated, his face
much discoloured; there was also a severe contusion above the
eye and a large tumour on the right thigh.' After treatment he
was 'removed in a post-chaise to Leeds where he remained

under the care of Mr Petty, a medical man, for two months, who after that time, recommended him to go to Blackpool for ... the sea air. After remaining there for some time, he returned home somewhat better and ... was enabled to attend to business, but had not yet recovered the use of his arm.'

The mail had been racing another coach — the *Independent*.[21] Racing killed and injured many travellers. When there were two coaches working the same ground coachmen's orders were often 'Be first'. Even without this injunction there was a tendency to race.

According to Corbett, in reminiscences of his driving days, accidents from this cause were greatly exaggerated. When coaches were running strong opposition, he argued, everything, horses, coach and harness, was the very best, and only real 'artists' would be put on the box. There was usually a code of conduct within which coachmen raced each other. Neck-and-neck races were rare, except occasionally when the road was wide enough. Usually coachmen did not try to give one another the 'go-bye' unless the leading coach stopped, say to pick up or put down a passenger. It was understood that the one stopped would pull over, leaving space to pass. Once past, the other would 'spring 'em' to try to 'change' and be off again without being passed. 'None,' added Corbett, 'but the most reckless raced downhill.'

Judging by accident reports this is a great deal less than the truth. There were many more reckless drivers than Corbett implies. One enthusiast, Lord Algernon St Maur, later Duke of Somerset, did admit, 'Some of these men were terribly reckless'. They put their passengers' lives at risk both by racing downhill and by trying to 'block' the pursuing coach, as in 1826 when the *Champion*, driven by one Scott, was pursuing the *Express*, driven by Samuel Scott, towards Liverpool. The *Champion* was overhauling the *Express* outside the Turk's Head, Knotty Ash, when Sam Scott pulled his leaders across, jamming the *Champion* against some carts, resulting in two of the horses being badly injured.[22]

In 1838 a tussle had been going on for some time between two rival Leeds–London coaches, *Courier* and *Express*, the latter seemingly having the edge. The *Courier's* proprietors hired Richard Rothwell to drive the coach in 'quicker time',

The 'go-bye'

and on the 17 July he was making a particularly determined effort. He told ostlers at the Golden Lion, Leeds, that
he 'would show the Express the hind boot before ...
Wakefield'.

The *Express* was first off and the *Courier* sped after it, too
hastily for Emanuel Ewthwaite, a linen weaver. 'I spoke to the
coachman several times .... At one time I begged of him
when driving very furiously not to go so fast, and he slackened
his speed a little.' Coming up Belle Hill (where William
Herfield had died), Rothwell played his hand and began to over-
haul the *Express* until both teams were galloping side by side.
Ewthwaite again begged Rothwell to slow, which he did, but
mainly because several coal carts appeared and he nearly ran
foul of them. The *Express* pulled away and remained tantalisingly in view 400 yards ahead.

The *Express* horses now on their mettle, Watson was having
difficulty controlling them and a passenger had to help hold
them back. He deemed it wise to put the 'slipper' on at
Lofthouse Hill, near Wakefield, although it was not usual

practice. The *Courier* gained ground, for Rothwell deigned to put *his* slipper on and plunged downhill in hot pursuit.

'Michael,' shouted Jeremiah Stocks, his guard, 'take time, go carefully down.'

Rothwell did hold the horses well back on the steepest pitch, but then let them go. The *Express* appeared and disappeared tantalisingly ahead. The *Courier* was gaining. Rothwell knew the *Express* must stop to let George Edridge, the guard, take off the skid, and he prepared to give Watson the go-bye.

Watson had a trick up his sleeve and stopped a little farther on than usual, hidden from view and so far out in the road as to be virtually on the wrong side. Edridge snatched off the slipper as the *Courier* appeared fifty yards behind, and Watson began to pull out even before his guard was aboard.

Rothwell was faced with a sudden quandary. Impossible to pull up before he was on the *Express*; no room to overtake on the right, because the rival coach was on the wrong side; only a narrow and narrowing gap on the left.

'Mind, George!' screamed the *Courier*'s guard as they galloped almost up to the *Express*, where Edridge was just climbing up. This made Rothwell's mind up for him. He swung his team to the left and immediately overturned the coach. Mrs Morelle was flung off and killed; others were injured. A verdict of manslaughter was returned against Michael Rothwell at the inquest.[23]

Of course, it was really up to coachmen's employers to dismiss them for racing and furious driving, and some did, — but rarely, because they had often given the order to 'Be first'. What got men dismissed was coming unstuck and having a smash.

Otherwise proprietors were determined their coach must be fastest against any opposition. It was partly pride and honour — 'in a case where your *honour* like is concerned proprietors don't stick at trifles', said one coachman. The *Pilot* and *Telegraph* ran in spirited opposition between Leeds and Birmingham. Four Methodist ministers, whose journey to the Methodist Conference in Leeds had been accomplished in 'a very violent and dangerous manner' on the *Telegraph*, begged the proprietor, Matthew Outhwaite, himself a staunch Leeds Methodist, to admonish coachman, Tom Johnson, and warn him against the evils of racing. 'Now, Tom,' said Outhwaite heavily, in the hearing of the clergy. 'No racing on any account, mind you, or I'll discharge you.' Then, more quietly, 'And I'll discharge you, too, if you dare to let the *Pilot* beat you to Wakefield!'[24]

The redoubtable Ann Nelson is reputed to have retorted to one driver who came in second, protesting he had wanted to spare the horses, 'I'll not fail to find horseflesh, and I look to you to drive. If you let any other coach pass you, no longer shall you drive for me!' Some top drivers were offered huge sums to come over and see off the opposition. It was rumoured Richard Blight was promised £12 a week by a Bristol proprietor to drive for a competitor. He declined. All sorts of tricks were resorted to — 'passing and repassing, cutting and slashing, tipping over and tipping under, wrong doings and right doings . . ., lawyers and lawsuits, glory and defeat'. In one frantic competition in Devon the coach in front would drag a cluster of thorn bushes to raise the dust. Some really dirty campaigns involved tampering with linchpins![25]

People along the route enjoyed contests hugely, turned out to watch, even laid bets on who would be first. Of course, they were not on the coaches, but many travellers too preferred the fastest coach. As a sailor remarked about the speed of a coach which had crashed, 'I wasn't aware . . . he drove too fast for me; I wished him to get on as fast as he could, as I wanted to get to the end of my journey.'[26]

Yet, very often, furious racing was quite unnecessary. Following Mrs Morelle's death a local newspaper railed against 'recklessness . . . displayed by the proprietors of some coaches in Yorkshire . . . especially the furious opposition . . . running from Leeds to Birmingham'. Good speed could be attained over a long journey 'without such galloping', as was demonstrated by the Halifax mail — 'the fastest coach in this part of the kingdom, and yet perfectly safe'. And there was a limit to how far ahead of schedule a long-distance coach could get. It merely finished up at certain staging points waiting its 'proper and usual time'.[27]

Still, but for the spirit that racing engendered Bianconi might have failed. His first car, from Clonmel to Cahir, was unsuccessful. People were used to walking and continued to do so. 'Bian' started a cheaper opposition car, keeping ownership secret even from the drivers. The excitement of the contest and the cheapness of the fare soon filled both cars. Bianconi had put an expensive yellow horse on the competing car. One evening his driver came in proudly: 'You know the great big yallah horse under the opposition car. Well, sir, he'll niver run another yard. I broke his heart this night. I raced him in from beyant Moore o'Barns, and he'll niver thravel agin.' Bianconi had to show delight, but he ended competition there and then, the place of cars in Irish history assured.

'His first car was unsuccessful.'

5

CUTTERS AND CADS

Accounts of coaching usually focus on the 'long' coach, with its romance of the open road, high speeds, faraway places . . . There were in fact probably as many coaches involved in the 'short stage' system, where slower vehicles, usually pulled by two horses, filled in gaps at angles and even parallel to main coach routes.

The largest number of short-stage coaches came to operate in and around London as the middle classes, growing in wealth and number, moved out to suburbs like Paddington (and beyond), and needed transport to their place of business. By 1825 there were perhaps 600 London short-stages making around 1,800 journeys daily, accounting for about a fifth of *all* stagecoaches in the country.[1] If the 'long' coach system was hardly the 'perfection' claimed, the London short-stage verged on chaos.

It grew rapidly from 1815 — too rapidly for narrow streets and narrower regulations. The hackney coaches (the taxis of the day) had established a monopoly on 'the stones' — the setts which served as carriageway in the City and the borough of Southwark. Consequently short-stages could only drop off and pick up in central London at their City termini. Any violation of 'Taylor's Act' in plying for passengers, or even lingering above five minutes in forbidden territory, and coach and horses were taken off to the pound — the Green Yard. Their return cost £6, causing some scenes of anguish and altercation.

Forbidden to linger on the stones, even at termini, coachmen were harassed — as ever-increasing numbers of coaches came to block up streets and prevent customers coming to shops in their carriages. Horses left evidence of their stay in abundance (more acceptable, apparently, from carriage than from coach animals). In 1822 there were complaints of the 'nuisance . . . daily and all day long taking place in the north side of St Paul's churchyard [the main City terminus] by the number of stage coaches stopping'. The Lord Chief Justice thundered that 'no one had the right to make a public stable of the King's highway'; more doses of the dreaded Green Yard were handed out, but the evil continued. There was nowhere to go until improvements to main thoroughfares, in the 1820s, began to alleviate the problem.[2]

If stationary coaches disturbed the citizens, moving ones enraged them. Coachmen would insist on copying their 'long' colleagues in racing even in the narrow, crowded, often badly maintained city thoroughfares. It was particularly dangerous for pedestrians. When an old man got knocked down in Aldgate in 1825 one inhabitant gave evidence: 'The contest between the drivers was a desperate one, and indeed neither old nor young had any chance of escaping with whole bones whenever these vagabonds who drove the Blackwall stages took it into their heads to race against each other.'[3]

It was a cut-throat business. Although there were substantial proprietors, many coaches were operated by men who owned one or two, often driving one themselves. As more coaches came into operation competition was sharp; passengers were at a premium. They raced principally to get first to passengers, but there was an element of daring-do. Thomas Warner, driver of an Acton stage, kept passing Vauxhall's coach (driven by staid old Mr Vauxhall), at speed, crossing the horses' heads repeatedly, crowing like a cock to shouts of 'Go it, go it'.[4]

Short-stage coachmen did not enter into the more gentlemanly spirit of 'long' coach races. It was a serious business and the gloves were off. Their character often left much to be desired. Dickens illustrated how mail and long coachmen looked down on short-stage drivers. 'It was wery wulger to write Potry,' Weller told Sam. He 'never knowed a coachman write Potry, except vun as wrote a most affecting copy o' werses the night afore he was hung: but then he vos only a Camberwell man — so that says notting.'

The worst villains were based not at Camberwell but at

Paddington, followed closely by Blackwell coachmen, the two
places where most coaches started — fifty-four and twenty-
nine in 1825. One magistrate complained in 1826 how 'these
Paddington stage coach drivers had . . . become an absolute
nuisance . . . from their violence and quarrelling', and another
expressed his abhorrence of 'the outrageous malicious and
violent conduct of some . . . Paddington drivers'.

They hurled insults at each other — and worse. As John Cox
passed the Angel, Islington, Henry Gulliver was waiting. 'I'll
be one with you before I get to Paddington,' he snarled. 'I'll
either pull your head off or smash your coach.'

Sure enough, near Marylebone turnpike he whipped up and
drove against Cox's coach with such violence as to force it
against the gatepost, throwing off two passengers and Cox.
Three months later, as Richard Fell drove Bull's coach along
Paddington Street, Gulliver and Chandler began pelting him
with stones, threatening to 'cut his bloody nose off'. Fell
confessed himself 'afraid to drive . . . from the violence of
these men . . .'.

Drink played its part. William Chandler ('The Cutter')
knocked down a horse with his pole and nearly killed a boy.

'How can I help it?' he told an outraged outside passenger.
'I'm not fit to drive. Master kept me up all night and made me
drunk.'[5]

The denials and excuses make interesting reading. Henry
Coxeter, another Paddington coachman, was charged with
furious driving.

Coachman: 'Why, I say as how my horses was not galloping
whatever; one horse was trotting, you must know, your
worship, and the little brown mare was cantering.'

Mr Griffith: 'Cantering is galloping.'

'Oh, no, it ain't; my little mare can't trot out of a walk, and
she can't gallop at all.'

'It's all nonsense; this gentleman says you was racing.'

'Don't you see, sir, I pushed on to get round t'other coach,
and pulled up in the clean.'

'That is no excuse; you should have waited half a minute,
and let the other coach pass.'

' 'Pon my honour, sir, the gentleman's mistaken; my mare
can't gallop, she's been used to carry a lady, and she's rather
groggy.'

'Groggy! I thought you was speaking of a horse.'
'Yes, sir, of my little brown mare; she is groggy.'
'Your mare groggy! What do you mean, man? Do, pray,
speak to be understood.'
'Why, sir, when a horse is shook afore, and lame a' both legs,
we call 'em groggy, and they can't gallop.'
Fined 50s and costs.

One owner swore his coach was not galloping, whereupon
the magistrate retorted, 'We know the coach couldn't gallop;
but we have sufficient evidence to show that the horses did.'
Another defendant 'had two "very spirity horses" and they
would "go" in spite of his teeth'.[6]

Even when coaches skidded to a halt where passengers
waited, the fun was not necessarily over. One court case 'arose
out of one of those disgraceful contests for passengers . . . daily
occurring'. Both John Glover and James Earl plied from the
Flower Pot, Bishopsgate Street. A couple were about to board
Glover's coach when Earl endeavoured to persuade them on to
his. Glover pushed him aside. Earl struck him 'a most violent
blow, the effects of which he felt for a long time'. There was
clearly much pent-up frustration behind it, since Earl claimed
'he had to work against four . . . men, who were in the habit of
telling everyone that his coach was the wrong one'.[7]

Not that drivers of the shortest-distance coaches (as from
Paddington to the Bank) usually got involved in physical dis-
putes over passengers. This usually involved their 'cads', boys
or young men who let passengers in and out and attended to
parcels. Cads were also expected to seek out and entice
passengers aboard. These 'busy, impertinent, resolute' fellows
were considered the lowest of the low — 'a species of saucy
thieves, who, whenever they had an opportunity of plundering,
committed plunder without remorse'. They were paid by the
coachman, about 1s 6d a week and sometimes a share of the
parcel profits.[8]

Once aboard, passengers were often treated in cavalier
fashion. Any sort of criticism was fatal. Martin Foster detailed
an exchange with a Greenwich coachman in 1824. They
trotted along at a tolerable pace to Bricklayer's Arms, then
came to a full stop. After five minutes Foster inadvisably said,
'Come, coachee, are you going on?'
'Yes, in a few minutes,' was the careless reply.

London short-stage, showing the 'busy, impertinent, resolute cad'
by the 'dickey' and coachman suitably insolent. *British Railways
Board and Birmingham Public Libraries*

Another five minutes passed and Foster repeated the
question.

'In a few minutes, sir,' was the surly reply. 'I'm allowed ten
minutes.'

'Well, you've already been above that time, and if you don't
go on I shall get out and walk.'

'You may walk and be damned, but I'll have my fare to
Greenwich.'

Foster made to get down, but the coachman, Joseph Waters,
seized his coat lapels threateningly.

'Please to hand over my eighteenpence first?'

'Will you take me to Greenwich?'

'Yes,' said Waters, the truth coming out. 'When my coach is
full.'

Foster began to climb down.

'Come, come, at any rate you're not going to cheat me out of
your ride here.'

'I don't mean to cheat you, but if you don't proceed I shall try to punish you and fine you 40s.'

'Forty shillings,' replied Waters 'that's a good one,' adding with an oath, 'Do you think forty shillings anything to me?' — indicating either bravado or, despite all the problems, that short-stage economics were perhaps not so desperate.

The final shaft of repartee 'produced a great laugh among the coachmen and caddees, who had now gathered around', assailing Foster insolently, and he deemed it prudent to climb back in. It was 'so precisely a description of the everyday's occurrences on the Greenwich road' and of the 'general insolence of the coachmen so proverbial.'[9]

Captain Johnson spoke out of turn to James Rowe, who drove like fury from Kew Bridge to Piccadilly. Rowe immediately ordered him off (claiming he was not driving to town with one passenger) turned round and headed back. Johnson stayed on for some way, but eventually got off and was obliged to walk back. Harsh words were exchanged, and it might have ended violently except, the Captain claimed, 'you durst not for the fear of a good threshing. It was my *inches* that protected me, my hearty.'[10]

Frequently, when there were few passengers aboard, drivers simply refused to take them on to St Pauls, since there was no hope of picking up more on the 'stones'. They simply turned round and passengers had no choice but to get off. There would have been more complaints, but, as 'Publicus', also ditched at Piccadilly, explained, he was, like many others, unable to 'spare the time which would be requisite to the seeking of redress, and must therefore put up with the imposition ...'.[11]

High hopes were raised when George Shillibeer introduced the omnibus from Paris, in 1829, to run from Paddington to the Bank. It would be safer, more regular and more respectable than the coaches. Shillibeer's buses *were* well run. He selected his men carefully, especially the *conducteurs*, two of whom were sons of naval officers. Unfortunately they were so successful (although Shillibeer eventually failed) that new evils (and many old ones) reappeared.

Short-stage people were unhappy with the new rival, of course. The 'Paddington coachmen rejoiced much' when they heard of an accident to Shillibeer's omnibus, and there was some misconduct, but their animosity was dwarfed by that of cabmen from 5 January 1832, when omnibuses (and short-stages) were allowed to pick up on the stones. The New Stamp Act lost cabmen their monopoly. Wyburn, 'A well behaved man', one of Shillibeer's conductors, complained of 'hourly insults he received on passing the different coach [cab] stands . . . and said that so long as the drivers confined themselves to abuse only he did not care', but one morning a cab driver pelted him with dirt, liberally spraying passengers inside. When Wyburn complained, cabmen followed the omnibus, calling him the 'grossest names and much abused him'. A tradesman 'frequently witnessed the blackguard conduct of the hackney drivers towards Shillibeer's omnibus'.[12]

The omnibuses' very success brought other problems. As Thomas Haydon, an omnibus proprietor in the Mile End Road, was reported in 1834: 'About two years ago he commenced running an omnibus from the west-end . . ., and he felt great benefit . . . but . . . he had in a short time to encounter a sharp opposition 'and instead of just his omnibus starting six times, numbers increased to ninety-five times a day. This created 'a nuisance that was almost intolerable and complaints were almost hourly made . . .'.[13]

Short-stage proprietors, seeing omnibuses were unbeatable, joined them. Coaches disappeared; omnibuses appeared like mushrooms. Sharp competition between coaches transferred to them. Coachmen and cads, including the most disreputable, transferred too. Because of the surplus of omnibuses and the taxation system, passengers remained at a premium. In one 'disgraceful scene' a couple of servant girls were almost torn apart by two Chelsea bus conductors near Chancery Lane. As they made to board one bus 'the rival manager immediately descended from the step . . . to persuade them to take . . . his vehicle'. There followed 'a warm altercation between these conductors who behaved in a most insolent and indelicate manner towards these unprotected females, by pulling and dragging them towards their separate omnibuses, until their clothes were most shamefully disfigured'. In the end the girls took neither. 'Both vehicles then went off in a gallop . . . to the imminent danger of everybody . . ., the drivers blackguarding each other down to Charing Cross, with the foulest of language, and the most disgusting distortions of countenance. When will these ruffians be taught better manners, and at least put a bridle upon their tongues and spare the feelings of the female part of their company?'[14]

Dickens reckoned the omnibus cad's greatest boast was 'he can chuck an old gen'lm'n into the buss, shut him in, and rattle off afore he knows where it's a-going to'.[15] The name 'cad' remained some time before the French *conducteur* caught on.

Omnibus design introduced rear loading, making possible a new little game — 'poling'. This involved running so close to a preceding bus that when both stopped the pole between the two horses behind prevented people from mounting the one 'in front' and passengers were thus captured by the second. In one incident a Mile End omnibus, driven by Samuel Cable, 'poled' the Chelsea *Time Flies* through the Poultry, Cheapside and St Paul's churchyard, 'twice baulking passengers from getting into the *Time Flies*, and catching them himself'. William Stevens, the conductor, protested as they went down Ludgate Hill. Cable threatened to whip him and came so close the pole struck Stevens's legs, knocking him off the 'monkey board'.

Poling was particularly dangerous at speed. Before stopping a driver was supposed to hold up his whip as a signal. This was not always forthcoming, especially during sharp opposition. In one incident the front vehicle suddenly stopped, after moving at 'a furious rate' and 'the pole of the hind omnibus struck the conductor across the legs with such tremendous violence . . . it fractured his leg in a shocking manner'.[16]

When not 'poling' they were, often as not, racing, partly to get to passengers first and then keep in front by various devices — 'cutting and crossing' and generally weaving about down the busy street — partly for the sheer hell of it, and partly, one suspects, because they were often drunk. One driver, 'evidently more than half intoxicated', swore he would keep ahead of a rival and 'began to lash his horses violently to the top of their speed' until they were so exhausted they stood 'panting and trembling'. 'The other omnibus darted up and there not being sufficient space to push ahead, it dashed against the former with a fearful shock, and turned it on one side, unseating the passengers and throwing one of the horses.'

A *conducteur* on his 'monkey board'. *British Libruary Newspaper
Library*

Another race between Camberwell omnibuses caused such a
smash that one was lifted on to the footpath. One of the
horses, forced against a lamp post, was killed. Two buses
racing for the Green Man turnpike in the Kent Road arrived
simultaneously. 'The crash was terrific.'[17]

Surprisingly few passengers were killed or injured. Omnibuses were sturdily built and there were no passengers on top
at first, but fears must often have been tremendous. John
Robertshaw, a linen draper, climbed aboard a Paddington bus
which was soon over-full, causing 'the greatest annoyance and
inconvenience, from the manner ... they were crowded
together'. The passengers complained vigorously to John
Boissonade, the driver, but he 'commenced pouring forth a
volly of the foulest abuse, and suddenly stopping, took up a
man in a beastly state of intoxication, who had no sooner

tumbled in than he raised his fist and assaulted a middle-aged gentleman without the slightest provocation by striking him a desperate blow on the eye'. There was, understandably, a 'scene of indescribable uproar and confusion' in the bus, added to by Boissonade lashing his horses with all his might 'regardless of the screaming of the ladies and loud remonstrances of the other passengers, who every moment dreaded ... some serious accident ...'.

Boissonade eventually pulled up, and a woman carrying an infant in her arms, 'in almost a fainting state, from the terror and alarm into which she had been thrown', pressed to get out. 'For God's sake take my money and let me out!' She had just made the steps when the 'brutal fellow' whipped up, throwing woman and child head first into the road. The omnibus careered along, horses galloping 'as fast as they could lays legs to the ground'. Robertshaw, convinced that 'nothing short of a miracle would prevent ... a frightful collision', jumped out behind 'at the imminent risk of his life'. He rushed forward to seize the reins, but Boissonade began lashing his arm furiously with the whip. He had to let go and narrowly escaped being trampled on and run over.[18]

William Everest was another 'out-and-outer'. In 1839 he had Elizabeth Baxter as a passenger beside him on a Kennington omnibus. He 'began to conduct himself towards her in such an indecent manner ... that she requested to be set down and resisted his attempts to pull up her clothes', but he drove on, whereupon she threatened to call out. 'Then I'll throw you off,' he said, and, good as his word, lifted her up and threw her into the road.

Off duty they could be as brutal as on. A Paddington driver, father of Maria Martin, had at one time left her destitute and later had flogged her unmercifully until she fainted. The flesh was actually cut out. George Hoby, another of the London Conveyance Company's Paddington drivers, had flown into a violent passion when asked for arrears of rent and struck his landlord several times with a large key, laying his forehead open. 'A delicate-looking young woman ... ascended the witness box; she stated that she had been married three or four years to the prisoner, by whom she had six children; he was in the habit of cruelly ill-using her, and on Thursday night last, while she was eating some oysters for supper, he said he hoped they would stick in her throat and choke her. He then struck her a violent blow, which gave her a black eye.'

Not that these men were always so manly. Frederick Oddy, a Blackwall conductor, in an altercation with a passenger had said the worst that could happen to him was a fine 'and for that he cared little', but when the magistrate threatened him with the treadmill 'the defendant began to blubber'.[19]

Robert Horne was murdered by a pack of six Paddington omnibus men.[20] With such men at the reins, accidents to pedestrians were frequent. When a little girl was killed several jurymen remarked, 'it was no uncommon thing to observe three of them racing abreast at . . . ten to fifteen miles an hour' between Islington and the Bank.[21]

All else was forgotten in the fury of these races. An argument between conductors of the *Emperor* and *Dart* Paddington omnibuses in 1836 caused a fearful race which killed Leonard Coleman, a corn and coal merchant. The *Dart*, driven by John Edwards, made to pass when George Poole on the *Emperor* whipped up his horses and 'acted in strong opposition, and drove at a furious rate for a considerable distance'. Coleman, approaching on horseback, was unable to get out of the way. Sandwiched between the two, he was knocked from his horse and killed. Neither driver took the 'least notice of the accident' but whipped on their horses, going neck-and-neck down the street, twice passing habitual stopping places. Most of the alarmed passengers escaped as best they could. Several fell down on to the road. The buses thrashed on regardless, not stopping until Euston Square.[22]

Fines had little effect. William Quantill, driver of one of Collier's Hammersmith omnibuses, had sworn a solemn 'vow in heaven' and took 'his davy he'd never gallop nor whip his 'osses agin whatsomdever' but was spotted racing a Brentford bus through Knightsbridge at a tremendous rate. Apparently drivers contributed 1s a week to a common fund used to pay fines, and although court cases were frequent enough they hardly represent the ubiquity of offences. One magistrate reckoned that 'informers were paid to wink at these abuses, therefore the cases seldom come before a magistrate'.[23]

Proprietors encouraged drivers and conductors in their

unpleasant activities, but the more respectable recognised the folly of such raw competition. George Shillibeer proposed a reduction in the number of omnibuses to fifty-seven on the Paddington–Bank route (already ninety by September 1831) and that they should run regularly every three minutes, with officers to regulate and restrain racing and poling.

The plan was acted upon, with consequent improvements. Other agreements (sometimes by forming companies) on other routes at various times did bring similar order. But such attempts could be short-lived. New proprietors, not party to the agreement, started and the whole chaotic process began again. And there was always the human element. A magistrate remarked, after a spirited race by James Pool, driver of a Paddington omnibus, that 'scarcely a week passed without some driver belonging to the new company [the London Conveyance Company] (who in the onset of their career had led the public to imagine their best exertions should be used to reform all pre-existing abuses . . .) being brought up for furious driving, or other occurrences; the former offence was of almost hourly occurrence . . .'.[24]

The Omnibus Act of 1838 did bring further improvement (with regulations on overcrowding, licensing of vehicles and personnel, etc.), more associations were formed, but complaints if abated did continue. The London General Omnibus Company, a French concern formed in 1855, bought out six hundred of the existing eight hundred or so omnibuses, and by creating a monopoly on many routes reduced the problems caused by acute competition. But again not for long, since new competitors entered the fray once more, patriotically trading on the intrusion of the 'French Monopoly', and even after the LGO Co became a British concern in 1859 competition continued.

Still, for all the problems, the boon omnibuses brought cannot be denied, which is no doubt why their quirks were tolerated. As 'A Traveller' conceded in 1835, after complaining bitterly of congestion, especially at tradesmen's doors, of the 'scandalous manner in which omnibuses are now conducted', of 'inconvenience and danger', nonetheless the 'accommodation afforded by them of a drive from one extremity of this vast metropolis to the other for 6d, and the time thereby gained by a great number . . . compelled to go all that way on foot if they had to pay a higher price . . ., are certainly very material considerations in favour of omnibuses'.[25]

Omnibuses in Fleet Street, 1848. *British Library Newspaper Library*

6

DELAY, EXTORTION AND HIGHWAYMEN

Passengers were not the only ones to complain.

'Oh, Blyth, you have my guns all right?' an eager sportsman called to the *Mazeppa*'s guard as it rolled into Hereford.

'No, sir,' replied the guard sheepishly. 'Your guns went off in Gloucester. In going over the rough stones your case lay on the roof . . ., fell off, and, I'm sorry to say, was all broke in a hundred pieces.'

'Careless fellow!' shouted the angry gent. 'What am I to do, and tomorrow first of September? Well, I shall expect you to pay for your carelessness.'

The Hereford man was not alone. Squire Villebois, master of the Hampshire hunt, was equally eagerly awaiting a valuable stock foxhound from the Earl of Shrewsbury. John Bayzand, disliking the look of the dog's hamper, put it in the rear boot for safety. At Abingdon there was a large hole and no hound.

The squire was waiting at Sandleford Priory. 'Good morning, Bayzand. You have my hound safe, I hope?'

'No, sir, I'm sorry to tell you I put him in the hind boot for security, and he gnawed his way out.'

'Well, I'm very much annoyed and disappointed. I shall expect you to pay for it. I can assure you the dog [is] very valuable.'[1]

Unfortunately it was not just the odd sportsman who was disappointed. Coaches were important transporters of goods — light, high-value goods like banknotes and bills of exchange, jewellery, game, certain types of ironmongery, fashionable articles like silk haberdashery — carried on a regular basis. The Kidderminster–London coach regularly carried large quantities of needles despite the weight.[2]

Merchants used coaches because their goods were in urgent demand, and they were prepared to pay high charges to see them off smartly and safely. It cost £1 to send a small box of needles. Richard Westall, a Birmingham linen draper, reckoned it cost 8s 4d per cwt compared with 5s by waggon in carrying *his* supplies from London in 1832. But coaches were relatively small. Frederick Barnes, a wholesale ironmonger, in London and Birmingham, often had packages refused. 'Mr Barnes,' the bookkeepers told him, 'you wouldn't like to travel in a coach with 800 or 900 lbs on the top of it or in the boot.' He missed orders and shipments in consequence. The cost and delay had been a 'considerable embarrassment' to him. In fact 'it has been the ruin of our business', he complained.[3]

Not that charges were always as advertised. Mr Witson disputed a charge of 3s 2d for a game basket brought by the Fakenham coach to the Golden Cross in 1822. He should, he claimed, have been charged by weight at 2d per lb as advertised. The inn representative urged 'the rule of charging by weight was by no means general or compulsory, and . . . not applicable to small parcels instancing . . . attorney's papers, which perhaps did not weigh above half a pound, and asked whether it would reasonably be expected, after bringing such papers 300 or 400 miles . . . that the charge . . . be only 1d. Game in particular, he said, was never charged by weight . . .'. The magistrate gave him to understand it should be. Whereupon he 'protested loudly against the principle of such a decision'.[4]

Cost of delivery was another sore point, especially in London, where again considerable latitude was taken by inn-keeper/coachmasters. In return for a delivery monopoly, porterage charges were fixed by the London Porterage Act, 1799 — for instance, the delivery charge for a parcel under 50 lb within a quarter of a mile was 3d. Why then did Mr Roach, living very close to the White Horse Inn, Fetter Lane, have to pay 4d? William Bales, bookkeeper at the inn, tried to justify the charge 'on the ground of the uniform practice of doing so for the last twenty years' but the magistrate was unimpressed.[5]

Delays in delivery were particularly upsetting. Mr Minns was understandably annoyed when four ducks and a goose spoiled. Arriving at the Swan with two Necks the night of

27 July, the basket did not reach him until the 29th. But there was no redress, since, at Hackney Field, he lived above half a mile 'beyond the stones'. Under the London Porterage Act terminal inns were obliged to forward goods to recipients within six hours of arrival, but only if they lived within half a mile of the 'stones'. Beyond that goods were delivered to subsidiary inns and, as the Swan bookkeeper explained, the basket had been sent to the Flower Pot, Bishopsgate Street, before noon on the 28th and the blame, therefore, rested there. To add to the confusion, the 'stones' had been extended since 1799, but the legal limit still lay where they had ended in that year.[6]

There was a complex sub-network of delivery services in London. Parcels for more far-flung places were taken from terminal inns to lesser establishments — taverns and smaller inns, in the City and West End — starting or calling places for short-stages, which carried them to further inns up to twenty miles out. For instance, in 1822 a game basket for Mr Tanner in Camberwell was brought by coach to the White Horse, Fetter Lane, and taken by porter to the King and Keys in Fleet Street for onward transmission by the Peckham short-stage, although Tanner complained it would have been quicker via the Green Dragon in Fleet Street to be forwarded by the Camberwell stage. At a few houses, where both long and short-stages called, there was a direct transfer from one system to the other — the Green Man and Still in Oxford Street being one example.[7]

Tanner's experience brings to light another imposition worked in over the years — 'a custom of long standing' — an agreement to charge a flat rate of 8d from inn to inn regardless of distance. Favourable to those liable for a charge of 1s 1d, say, it was less so for those who might pay 3d — like Mr Tanner — and it contravened the law.

Consumer resistance built up after the French wars as business incomes fell in deflationary times while coaching charges showed little tendency to fall with them. But such practices continued. In 1838 Mr Jackson was complaining of being overcharged for a parcel from Derby; Thomas Allen, surgeon at Mile End Road, of delay in delivery.[8]

These were not isolated incidents. 'Nothing in London is

worse executed or more dearly paid for than this service,' one bitter sufferer protested in 1837. 'Delay and extortion meet you on every occasion. When the legislature allowed six hours ... for ... delivery ... they never contemplated any right to the taking all that time by the innkeeper, except in cases of peculiar emergency. The public, however, not only very rarely obtain their parcels in less time, but are usually very fortunate

'Christmas time and the arrivals beyond all bounds'. The Norfolk coach arrives at Ann Nelson's Bull Inn, Aldgate. *British Library Newspaper Library*

if they get them in so little. There is always some ready excuse of large arrivals of grouse, solicitors' papers . . . and that it is Christmas time and the arrivals beyond all bounds.'

'This is far too bad,' he railed. 'The charge for the delivery of parcels is so high that there are thousands in London who would gladly perform this service with each separate parcel at the same rate; how exorbitant then must be the profit of the innkeeper upon his monopoly of delivery, far more than sufficient to enable him to let the public have their parcels in two hours instead of six, by the employment of more men and horses.'

Not that blame for exorbitant rates lay always direct with innkeepers and coachmasters. On a previous instance when overcharged for porterage from the White Horse Cellar, Mr Roach found the fault lay with the porters. In theory 'ticket porters' should have been the most honest men in London. They had to supply two respectable bondsmen to testify to character and supply a bond. The porter was issued with a badge signifying all was in order.[9] Unfortunately the badge holder was not always worthy of the trust.

The 'ticket fiddle' was rife among London porters and one of the fastest ways of making money short of stealing. It was simple enough. The bookkeeper, when giving the porter instructions, issued him with a ticket with carriage and porterage charges written in. The dodge was to alter the figures to a higher amount. 'It is a very pretty trade for you porters,' Alderman Waitham reproached Tomlinson, one of Waterhouse's porters, 'should you have fifty parcels to deliver of a day, to add an imposition of 6d upon each of them, thus to realise 25s.'

It was all a mistake, urged Tomlinson. Sometimes in the hurry of business, when bookkeeper and clerks were fully occupied, porters were obliged to fill in tickets themselves, and he had simply made a mistake.

'It is no mistake,' retorted the alderman. 'You know better, if is a fraud. This circumstance might be blown over the metropolis with a trumpet that every person may hear of it. It is a growing evil, and an example must be made.'

A Belle Sauvage porter faced the alderman's wrath a week later, getting 'an admonition which he will not be likely to forget' and a stiff fine, followed by Knight, of the Angel Inn, St Martins-le-Grand. Knight too insisted he had mistakenly written 3s 10d instead of 2s 10d at the bookkeeper's call, bringing forth another verbal lashing — 'offence notoriously practised, in one form or another, by all the porters of the metropolis', 'gross forgery and fraud', etc.[10]

The ticket fiddle went on, but porters became more cautious, the public more suspicious of alterations. The next dodge was for porters to lay hands on blank tickets and fill in their own figures. The art was, of course, to milk the receiver of a sum that made the risk worth while without so overdoing it as to cause him to complain and check with the office. Rogers, porter at the Old White Horse Cellar, Piccadilly, in 1823, *did* overdo it on a grand scale, stirring up eight complaints in one day. He was proved to have stolen some blank tickets even though the proprietors of the Cellar had 'with much care kept the printed tickets out of the reach of the porters . . ., in the fear that they would make an improper use of them'.

It seems to have acted as no great deterrent. Thomas Larkins, at the Green Man and Still, destroyed the ticket issued by the bookkeeper with a demand of 2d for carriage and porterage and fabricated his own for 2s 6d. The chairman of the Middlesex Sessions again drew attention to the 'notorious frequency of frauds of this kind' and gave him three months' imprisonment.[11]

The truth was, many people were too busy to contest charges and, grumbling, paid up, and continued to do as long as coaches ran. In 1838 they were still being subjected to the 'caprice of bookkeepers, cads, porters, and the like; and having to submit, in nine cases out of ten, to gross imposition, or else to lose time, and incur an infinity of trouble and expense in bringing the extortioner or his employer to justice'. Perhaps, too, many innkeepers and coachmasters turned a blind eye to irregularities unless public opinion became too forceful. Thomas Baskerville, porter at the Golden Cross, was convicted of taking excessive porterage in 1818. He was also convicted of charging carriage for a hare already paid for in the country. Nonetheless he was still porter at the Golden Cross in 1822.[12]

Then there was the story related by Dr Elliotson of St Thomas's, concerning James Adams, 'a squinting odd-looking fellow, aged forty-four' — occupation, coach porter. 'I ordered this patient ... another venesection ... on which day he begged me to show him such a little delicacy as a pheasant or a pigeon, and, on my telling him it was out of my power ..., he said that he did not mean that I should provide him with them, but if I would allow him to eat them, he would procure them himself. When I expressed my surprise ... he gave me a very cunning look, and said he was in the carrying line, took parcels from stage coaches to gentlemen's houses, and game among the rest; and that a pheasant or a pigeon or two could not help being lost now and then. I at once understood him but still there was this difficulty, that he was now in the hospital, and not engaged in practice.

' "Ah, but you know, sir," said he, "I've got several friends in the same line." '

'I, however, could not permit him to eat any sort of animal food, and between being tired of low diet and ashamed of what he had divulged, he disappeared before my next visit.'[13]

Another popular porter ploy was delivering dummy parcels — one so common that servants were given instructions not to pay charges on packets before examining the contents. Of course, London magnified the failings of the coaching industry, but similar malpractices went on, to a lesser degree, in the provinces. Brighton, for example, was as prone to dummy parcel deliveries as London.[14]

One consignment did go astray without complaint. It languished in the Castle coach office in Birmingham High Street. Clerks and porters became increasingly put out by 'strong and most disgusting effluvia'. Finally the 'loathsome smell' became unbearable and was tracked down to a large deal box which had been there more than two years. Inside were the remains of a human being in an advanced state of decomposition. Bodies were, in fact, a common illicit cargo on coaches. At a time when there was a shortage of corpses for dissection, organised companies, 'neither duly registered nor legally floated' — 'body snatchers' in fact — existed in different localities, to exhume newly buried corpses for despatch to London and Edinburgh teaching hospitals. Some West Country operatives forwarded the night's work in wooden cases as 'books'. The frequency and weight of the 'parcels' and

other circumstances aroused suspicion, one was opened and all
was exposed.[15]

Fiddles were not the prerogative of lower coaching orders
alone. Clerks and bookkeepers sometimes worked in collusion
with porters, and they had their own fiddles — one of which,
according to the *Taunton Courier*, was taking bribes from
coachmasters to direct parcels along more lucrative routes.
'Instances of this kind are continually occurring in this town,
wherein parcels, which ought to be sent by the Taunton coach
from London, are forwarded by the Bath or Bristol coach, and
then sent on by another conveyance, taxed with a charge
nearly double that which ought to be made. If this fraud is not
submitted to, the parcel is withheld.'[16]

Nor were coachmen and guards above 'making a bob or two
on the side'. Before the penny post was introduced in 1840,
sending (or, rather, receiving) letters was expensive, the charge
depending upon the distance, and it was common practice for
crews to carry them more cheaply. This upset nobody much,
apart from the Post Office, which then as now had a monopoly
of letter carriage. And one group of passengers actually benefited from the practice of 'shouldering', where short-distance
travellers on the road were charged a reduced fare, split
between driver and guard. Sometimes they were found out:

CAUTION TO STAGE COACHMEN
Last week Harry Watkins, driver of the Cambrian coach, between
Swansea and Cardiff, was convicted in the mitigated penalty of £5 for
defrauding the proprietors by carrying a passenger without entering his
name on the way-bill or paying his proper fare.[17]

Sometimes they were found out more dramatically. Henry
Gollan's indiscretion came to light when he stopped Green-
wood and Turner's *Prince Albert* at Besses o' the Barn, near
Manchester, to let out two insides. As he was mounting again
the horses set off at full speed and the coach overturned,
injuring most of the passengers. On investigation it was found
that it was carrying twenty-three instead of eighteen on the
waybill, and Henry was dismissed.[18]

Such practices were often tolerated if not overdone and came
close to being accepted as perks — but not quite. William
Chaplin's toast 'Here's to shouldering' at the coachmen's
annual May Day dinner has often been quoted. Less frequently

mentioned was the rider he added when cheers and laughter subsided — 'But don't let me catch you at it.'

Unfortunately there was more to it than the occasional pheasant disappearing, the odd passenger 'swallowed'. More substantial items 'fell off coaches'. George Weeks, horse-keeper at the Star inn, Andover, was attending the *Subscription* coach when he found a parcel. He quickly concealed it and later found it contained £200, which he 'put to his own use'. He was no hardened villain, became increasingly nervous, moved over to the White Hart and then joined the First Regiment of Royal Foot. But the 'circumstances lay so heavily on his mind ... he could rest neither night nor day' and ten years later gave himself up to justice.

In 1818 the Holyhead mail was repeatedly robbed, until guard Henry Harris was brought to trial. In 1838, when a box containing £900 in cash and £700 in bills disappeared, James Randle, the driver, and a 'cad', Worrall, were implicated.[19]

In 1822 John Baker, guard of the Exeter *Subscription*, was brought to trial for the robbery of £1,040. He had the parcel stitched into his pocket by a clerk at Sparke's Bank, Exeter. But soon after starting, Baker cut it out and stowed it in the seat, claiming later it was too burdensome for him to carry (although apparently he had frequently carried heavier parcels in hotter weather). At the Bull and Mouth, London, he 'discovered' the loss. Collusion seemed obvious, but all was not quite as it seemed, as the subsequent trial proved. Of course, there were dishonest people in coaching — one of Fagg's book-keepers, Joseph Smith, embezzled over £700 — and phenomenal amounts disappeared in transit, but it is not so certain coach people were any more dishonest — 'perks' aside — than the rest of the population.[20] The simple truth was there were rich pickings and they attracted the attention of outsiders.

Highwaymen and coaching have always made a romantic and exciting mixture, but the days of 'Stand and deliver' were long gone by 1815. Coaches went too fast and were too well guarded; roads much busier and speedier. A lone highwayman was at a serious disadvantage. There was still occasional armed robbery in Ireland, but even there robbers were obliged to hunt in packs, as when the Derry mail was attacked in 1823. Approaching Drogheda, Nugent, the coachman, perceived two drays and a ladder almost blocking the road, but seeing a gap he dashed the horses at it. A volley of about fifteen shots rang out, and a leader fell dead. Mackay, the guard, discharged his blunderbuss but a return of fire killed him. Once the guard had fallen the villains set about rifling the coach and passengers.

Money was not always the objective in Irish hold-ups. The following year the Cork–Dublin mail was stopped. Approaching the turnpike near Cashel, the gate was suddenly closed and the coach fired upon. The guard returned the fire. One horse was killed in the next volley and both guard and coachman wounded. The guard surrendered, but the attackers interfered with neither mail nor passengers and made off with the guard's firearms only! In the interminable family feuds and struggles against the subjugating British, arms were highly desirable items in troubled Ireland.

An attack on the Limerick–Waterford coach in 1822 near Tipperary had another objective.

'Put down the girl — put down the girl,' the armed attackers shouted in a determined manner. They took a young woman from the coach and made off.

Apparently she possessed a fortune of £200 and a man had endeavoured to force her into marriage, but she had escaped and he was awaiting trial at Clonmel, whither she was heading as chief witness. His friends reckoned eliminating her from the proceedings would do his case no harm, but after a gun battle with the Tipperary police she was retaken.

In Ireland the roads were in a poorer state than in Britain and less frequented. The Cork–Dublin mail in particular passed through some inhospitable places — 'loose and quaking bogs' — especially in winter. In February 1827 it was again fired on near Cahir at four o'clock in the morning but got safely through. In December it came under attack again in the same area. The coachman had been tipped off something was afoot as he left Johnstown. 'Take care of the bog', a man had whispered, but the coachman, thinking he was being warned not to get stuck, took little heed.

Near Cashel a shot rang out, and the ball actually passed through the coachman's hat and grazed the head of Somerset Townshend, a student at Dublin University, stunning him and setting his ear a-ringing. The guard blew his horn and distributed arms to the passengers, but the expected assault never came. A party of thirty men was passed on the road, and it was assumed that if the coach had stopped they would have fallen on it.

In Britain, if shots ever rang out as the coach passed, it was more likely to be an over-enthusiastic sportman than a highwayman, as when, in 1827, outside passengers on the Leeds–Manchester coach were sprayed with pellets near Dewsbury.[21]

Guards in Britain rarely drew their arms, let alone fired them. Moses Nobbs was one of the few who did, once, and he regretted it. One night early in his career, on the Bristol–Portsmouth mail, two men jumped out of a hedge, and caught hold of the horses.

'Look out! We're going to be robbed,' shouted the coachman.

Nobbs grabbed his blunderbuss, but the men ran off. He fired into the hedge. 'I don't know whether I hit anything; . . . but I do know that the recoil of the blunderbuss nearly knocked me off my seat. I've had many hard knocks in my time, but that blunderbuss kicked like a mule.'

Moses J. Nobbs, mail coach guard. *British Library*

If armed robberies were few, it does not mean there were no robberies. On the contrary, robberies of valuables in transit reached epidemic proportions in the 1820s and 1830s, accounting in aggregate for far more than highwaymen ever apportioned. Robbers became more prudent and sophisticated ... and effective as coaches carried increasing wealth, thus attracting the attentions of the 'Family'.

7

THE SWELL MOB, PETER-HUNTING AND THE KIDRIG

Passengers were robbed not at the point of a gun but discreetly as they waited at inns or even on the coach in the way the farmer returning from Beverley fair to Hull was almost robbed of £300 in 1825. He was sandwiched between two men who, engaging him in conversation, surreptitiously cut through his greatcoat into his breast pocket. They were successful, but fortunately he had secreted the money elsewhere.

Sometimes robbers jumped up to hang behind an unguarded coach, pretending to be porters. One woman, leaving London on the back of a coach where two men had hung for a time later discovered her cloak cut through, and her purse would have gone had not the clasp become entangled. 'Two rough-looking fellows' went too far on a Brighton coach. They began to cut through into an old lady's pocket, but unfortunately 'allowed the knife to penetrate even a little beyond'. She shouted, 'Thieves, murder,' and the robbers dropped off and ran away.

George Freestan's speciality was coaching inns, but he came unstuck in 1816 after robbing a passenger's clothing at the White Bear, Piccadilly, and received sentence of death at the age of twenty. Thomas Dale, fifty-two, had been found guilty the year before of stealing £14 from William Hone's greatcoat lying in the parlour of the Bull, Holborn.[1] Pickpockets were attracted to coach stations like flies to a jam pot. One gentleman alighting from an afternoon coach in Brighton was robbed of £66 and several bills of exchange, while another lost nearly £300 worth of cheques and notes.

Passengers in accidents could not always depend on protection. As Mrs Wood lay shocked and semi-conscious after the *True Blue* accident a woman stole her veil. Another 'monster in human shape' took the dead coachman's watch. After the Liverpool–Manchester *Doctor* came to grief in 1828, it was reported, 'a person who had assisted in conveying Miss Mitchell to the Woolpack had taken two or three rings from her fingers'.[2]

Then there were thieves who specialised in parcels. They ranged from petty thieves, always on hand to profit from carelessness on the part of coaching personnel, to 'rings' of high-class thieves and receivers for whom stagecoach robbery was big business.

James Hardy Vaux was not really a specialist in 'rumble-tumble' robbery but a petty crook who could turn his hand to most kinds of dishonest practice. He robbed a coach on impulse, but his experience demonstrates how easy it could be. 'After three days' amusement in Birmingham I again took coach, and having travelled all night was stopped about seven . . . at Henley-upon-Thames . . . I had been so free in my expenses at Birmingham, that I had . . . but four shillings left . . . . I therefore declined alighting . . . . It occurred to me that I had seen a number of small parcels put into the seats . . . and having frequently heard of large sums in banknotes being transmitted . . . , I was tempted to purloin one . . . . Without hesitation, then, I opened the seat, and taking out my bundle, untied it in case of surprise. As I had not time to examine the contents . . . [I] took out the first which came to hand.' He hid the prize in his own bundle, left the coach early and later found £47 9s hidden beneath a quantity of nails — a common ploy to disguise articles of value.[3]

Part of the trouble, as one man who had lost £2,000 explained, was that small parcels were often not even put under lock and key — '. . . no precaution is taken . . . and everyone accustomed to travel by mail must be convinced that every person who pays for an inside place can have ready access to the parcels placed in the seats: If one seat were regularly locked, and then entrusted solely to the guard, that would prove some security . . .'.

Fond hope! In 1820 the Bristol mail was robbed of parcels valued at nearly £400 by four men who booked the inside to themselves from Bath and, using a candle kindly supplied by the guard to 'pass away the time agreeably', had unlocked the box under the seat, broken the parcels' seals, taken out the cash, tied them up again and relocked the box. A 'patent lock of Bramah's manufacture' was no proof against thieves. In 1824 Thomas Faulkner, coachman to the Portsmouth *Hero*, took up a parcel of banknotes in Petersfield and put them in his own box seat, but on arrival at Gracechurch Street it was bare. From the lock protruded a skeleton key.

The following year a double lock and padlock failed to prevent robbers relieving the coachman's box of £2,040 on the London–Gravesend stage while he was 'taking refreshment'. In December 1824 the Stirling mail was robbed of £13,000 with consummate ease. A man boarded at Stirling as an outside passenger. The mail was followed closely by two men in a gig. At Kirliston the guard took the bags into the inn, leaving the mail box open. The outside passenger simply took out the parcels and made off in the gig with the loot, which was not missed until Edinburgh.[4]

Some specialists in 'rumble-tumble' robbery worked in a casual, opportunist way and were invariably caught in the end. They came to be well known — like the 'celebrated Crowder who gained much renown for coach robberies, and who is now transported' or William White, who got transported several times. But the more spectacular robberies were meticulously planned by skilled operators who were rarely caught. 'It is notorious that there exists a ... higher class of thieves and receivers,' a *Times* report of 1825 observed, 'several of whom are men possessed of considerable property, who direct their attention almost exclusively to this description of plunder; they are indefatigable in their exertions to obtain information ... and having concocted their plans ... with great art and caution, patiently await a favourable opportunity of effecting their nefarious purposes.' It was reckoned £500 had been spent and numerous journeys made over many months to bring off one big 'job'.

This was probably the robbery of the Ipswich mail of over £30,000 in 1822, which brought to light an interesting new twist. Alexander & Co., the Ipswich bank, sent considerable sums regularly between London and Ipswich by mail coach in a special strongbox. A clerk was employed to keep a constant eye on the box, but he did, on this occasion, pop out for a couple of minutes. The three other insides ripped the staple off the box and took the contents. One stayed on to Ipswich to engage the clerk in conversation so he would not examine the box.

The danger to the robbers came in trying to pass off the distinctive notes. The bank decided to issue new, red notes and requested the public to be wary of its black-ink notes. This prevented the gang making much use of their loot, but the business world was soon in chaos, as there was a 'general terror of the black Ipswich bank note'. The robbers' master stroke was to offer to return the notes for £6,000 in sovereigns and an indemnity from all charges. The bank offered £3,000 and eventually an understanding was reached.

This was not the first time. One magistrate complained that it had become too common, and solicitors had taken part in such 'disgraceful transactions' as go-betweens. 'What was to become of the justice of the country if its course was to be thus obstructed by men whose duty it was most peculiarly to aid it in its operations?'[5]

His words discouraged neither robbers nor negotiators, for shortly afterwards the Birmingham coach was robbed of over £7,000, probably by the same 'ring'. And when the Warwick mail was robbed in 1827 of £20,000, the *Times* reported, the thieves 'had resource to the usual mode of negotiating for its restoration .... The bankers were ... at first decidedly opposed to the "compromise", but as their business in ... Warwickshire had in great measure, become stagnant, owing to the inhabitants ... declining to take their notes, lest they ... become the holders of the stolen notes ... it was thought advisable ... to enter into the negotiations ... offered *sub rosa*, by the "family men" '. In the end it cost £2,000 to 'buy' back the booty.

Robberies on moving coaches obviously required much daring and iron nerve. Imagine engaging a clerk in conversation knowing at any moment he might discover you have robbed him of thousands of pounds! More thefts were made during the hustle and bustle of departure or arrival. The 'swell mob' 'invariably attended the departure of the mails'. The robbery of the Warwick mail, above, took place at Furnival's

Inn, Holborn, and that of the Birmingham in 1822 at the Swan with two Necks. The guard saw a man approach the coach, throw a coat across the seat as if intending to travel, then walk off.

'Who's that?' he asked.

'Why, he's a passenger of yours, to be sure,' replied the horsekeeper.

The guard got on with loading. He put two money parcels on the seat opposite the coat, intending to lock them up when he had a moment. Seconds later the parcels and greatcoat had disappeared. The mysterious man must have been watching every movement from a position in the busy yard.[6]

If villains often got information through constant observation they *were* sometimes assisted 'in their projects in obtaining intelligence, directly or indirectly, from unfaithful or incautious servants and agents', the *Times* reported. In 1824, when a box containing over five thousand guineas was sent to one coach yard for dispatch, a particularly 'strong muster of notorious characters and their satellites were observed near the yard . . .'. And how easy for a guard, by prior arrangement, to leave a parcel momentarily unguarded in just the right place, which is why John Baker, the Exeter *Subscription* guard, came, as we have seen, under considerable suspicion in 1822.

The coach reached the White Horse Cellar at about 6 p.m. Baker opened the door and, holding a light, checked the parcels. According to two women inside, a man looked in at the other window and spoke to him as if acquainted. The guard shut the seat and door. Soon afterwards the man returned and said, 'Give me that parcel.' Under the impression he was a porter, the women raised the seat and handed him the parcel. Baker was brought to trial along with thirty-seven-year-old William Thomas.

Fortunately for Baker, two public-spirited young brothers, Thomas and Phillip Dennis, came forward to let him off the hook. 'On the 6th December,' explained Thomas, '. . . I and my brother Phillip were going up to Holborn with some Waterloo crackers which we make — and in our way, saw the prisoner [Thomas] . . . with three others, at the Bell and Crown, Holborn; about the inn gateway. I had seen him before,

and stopped to notice him — we went and stood at Furnival's
Inn gate; I saw Thomas and his companions talking together
and *whipping* about the inn.' The three men took a hackney
coach and the brothers ran after it to Piccadilly, where 'just as
they got out, the Old Salisbury coach came up. Thomas was
then on the pavement — the other two crossed over to the Old
Salisbury coach . . .; one of the two men put on his greatcoat,
and appeared as if he was going off by the coach; but seeing the
Old Salisbury coach full inside, they went to another coach
which stood on the opposite side . . . the horses' heads . . .
towards the city. They went behind the coach . . . [and]
appeared to be assisting a lady out, and Thomas stood behind
them, with his face towards the coach door. I then went by,
and the guard stood against the hind wheel with a light in his
hand, looking over some boxes . . . . I . . . saw Thomas . . . go
up to the . . . coach . . . . I did not see him doing anything, but
he came away stooping . . . and appeared to be looking under
the coach — he went up a second time towards the coach door
. . . he then came back holding his hands in front, and . . . I
saw he had something white, which appeared to me to be a
parcel — the other two, who had been at the door, joined his
company.' When Thomas Rowe, a porter, admitted that
Thomas had asked him to go and change some of the notes for
sovereigns, the case against Thomas was complete. He was
found guilty and transported for seven years. Baker was
acquitted.[7]

Understandably, crews had mixed feelings about carrying
bankers' parcels. Although it meant extra money there was
always the risk of attack, or blame if they went astray. Bill
Bayzand, after one incident, finally refused to accept 'the very
great risk I ran in conveying safely bankers' parcels'.

One mail guard, who put a money parcel in his pistol holster
on the coach, got left behind. In a great fright, he ran and
walked a whole stage before catching up with his coach, by
which time the 'perspiration was oozing through his scarlet
coat'. At the end of the journey he sponged himself all over
with whisky, which apparently prevented any ill effects from
the exertion, though later in life he believed his health had
suffered because of it.[8]

Arrival and departure were busy times for guard or lone

coachman. It was difficult to have eyes everywhere, easy to be accused of carelessness after the event. Poor old William Wyatt, coachman of the Windsor *Union* for many years, lost his job when a £2,000 parcel went astray. The unfortunate man had received the attentions of a crook whose speciality was stage coach thefts — Billy White, 'Conky Beau' to his underworld friends. White no doubt knew Wyatt sometimes carried parcels, or he was tipped off. An accomplice, Roberts, shadowed Wyatt from the bank in Birching Lane, noting the type of parcel.

At the Gloucester Coffee House Wyatt put the parcel in the office 'while I looked out for my passengers. I then went in again and fetched this parcel out and gave it to Mrs Flowers [whom he had known many years] in the coach and told her to take great care of it, for it was of great value.'

Meanwhile Conky Beau had appeared at the coffee house door, a traveller's coat over his arm, as if preparing to take coach. The woman then heard White open the door. 'I looked round and he'd just got his hand on the parcel.'

'He said, "Here's my parcel, that's just right." '

'I said, "No, sir, it's Mr Wyatt's," and leaned towards the door.'

'He said, "Oh, no, ma'am, it's my parcel; it's all right," and he went away and shut the door.'

Despite an alibi from an ostler at an inn on the Maidstone road declaring White was dining there at the time, and in spite of the prisoner's own defence — 'I am totally innocent of this charge, as a child sucking at a woman's breast, oh my God' — thirty-six-year-old Conky Beau was found guilty and sentenced to seven years' transportation.[9]

Then there were those working the *kidrig* (defrauding porters of their loads by false pretences of various kinds) and *peter-hunters* who lifted parcels and trunks from passing carriages and stagecoach boots. For instance, in a dense December fog in 1818 thieves cut open the boot of the Windsor coach and stole all the parcels. Again, in November 1823 the Canterbury–London *Union* was robbed. 'The guard, hearing a noise . . . alighted to see if all was safe in the box behind. The night was very dark, but the guard, observing a man making away with a trunk, he immediately followed and secured him, when a determined scuffle ensued. The coachman, having placed the reins in the hands of a passenger, went to the assistance of his companion, and knocking the robber down, then secured him, as well as the horse and cart which had been deserted' by two other robbers.[10]

Peter-hunting was really a rural sport best carried out in dark, inclement weather, but there were London practitioners too. In January 1825 as the Holyhead *Hiberian* approached Piccadilly in driving rain Joseph Titmus, a cab driver, climbed up behind and laid hold of a box which he pitched into a chaise driven by Thomas Hatt, a servant 'out of place'. The guard saw nothing because he had covered his head with a large coat. Unfortunately for the two, three Bow Street officers saw them, took them into custody and also found a new saddle and bridle in the chaise which had earlier disappeared from the Horsham and Walton stage. Hatt was found to have a key that opened the rear boot. Both were transported for seven years.[11]

In the 1820s stagecoach robberies achieved epidemic proportions. In 1822 the Lord Mayor of London felt that 'The height to which the coach robberies were carried required . . . utmost exertions . . . by the magistracy'.[12] But still in 1825 a *Times* report reckoned that 'perhaps £100,000, transmitted by coaches, are known to have been stolen within the last few years'.

There may have been fewer robberies as the new Metropolitan Police began to get to grips with London crime from 1829 and indeed they probably saved Bill Bayzand being robbed. 'I shall ever remember one night in coming up Notting Hill, our bookkeeper from the Gloucester Warehouse Office, Oxford Street, got up behind and said quietly, ''Have you got a banker's parcel?'' '

'I said, ''Yes.'' '

' ''Then take care. I've two policemen at the office, and from the different moves and well-known bad characters about, you'd better take your banker's parcel in a cab at once to Lombard Street. I'll take charge of the passengers and coach.'' '

He delivered the parcel safely, 'taking a very great weight of responsibility and care from my mind. I shall not tell you the amount, for it was something immense. We found out, beyond a doubt, that a plan had been arranged to have the banker's parcel that night.'

It was probably too early for the police to have discouraged peter-hunters by January 1830, when Mr Drewe's maid, in watching the Brighton *True Blue* pass, noticed two men — Wildman and Harvey — hanging on to the back. She saw them open the boot and take out a large parcel and a brace of pheasants. Mr Drewe followed the men and detained them in spite of being beaten so vigorously by Harvey with the pheasants the heads came off in his hands.[13]

Thefts from around London inns do seem to have lessened in the 1830s, but robberies continued elsewhere. A particularly daring and astute one was carried out on the Edinburgh–Glasgow *Regent* in 1831. A box, chained and padlocked, holding £5,700 in banknotes and gold, was placed securely in the boot at Glasgow.

The coach started out empty inside, although fully booked. At Parkhead a man and woman boarded it to just past Airdrie. At Uphall a hole was discovered cut into the boot, chain and padlock wrenched off, money carefully sorted out from papers and gone. It turned out that six men had been involved, but the principal had been the woman, who was no woman at all but a coach proprietor — an 'inside job' indeed![14]

A similar technique robbed the Birmingham *Greyhound* of £420. At Coventry it was found that the only parcel of value had gone. Nothing else had been touched. 'The plan was, no doubt, deliberately laid, and the whole of the movements of the persons employed about the coach . . . watched. The exact place too in which the parcel was deposited must have been ascertained by the thieves, who were no doubt of the "London Family."'[15]

Until the end of coaching robberies continued, despite increasingly sophisticated means of protection. Five thousand pounds in notes and gold were placed in a box in the rear boot of the Manchester–Staffordshire *Potter* in 1839. A large chain running right round the coach, across the boot, terminated near the driver's feet. Nevertheless, in one of the most 'daring and audacious robberies', the box disappeared in the four miles between Macclesfield and Gosworth — the boot being completely broken open.[16]

One can understand the public's annoyance when goods and valuables failed to arrive. Coach proprietors *were* responsible for losses, but it was difficult to get recompense and usually involved resorting to law, where, generally, gross negligence had to be proved. And they refused to accept responsibility for items worth more than £5 'unless entered as such and paid for accordingly'. Many senders did not do this because the extra charge was high and it was thought to draw attention to a parcel's value, especially if packets were sent regularly. It was common practice to send valuables in ordinary-looking parcels in the hope that their innocent appearance would ensure immunity. It was often a vain hope.

Some felt the legal right enjoyed by carriers to limit their responsibility encouraged losses — 'the proprietors (being able to avoid responsibility beyond £5) are careless, and ... not sorry for an occasional loss, which creates alarm, and induces those who are obliged to send valuable parcels, to pay insurance, which is a source of very great profit to coach proprietors'.[17]

One judge at least sided with the public when he awarded compensation to a Coventry firm against the proprietors of a Liverpool coach when £146 worth of watches disappeared. Even though a large notice in the office warned of the proprietors' limited responsibility, and even though the firm had been sending valuable parcels for years without declaring them, the judge decided the senders had not been made fully aware of the carriers' limited responsibility.[18]

8

A VERY QUEER LOT

If danger in coaching came from mechanical and human failure
a third, substantial hazard came with the element that gave
coaching much of its charm — the horses. In the wild, a
horse's strongest defence is fleetness of foot. He tends to run
first, ask questions afterwards. Even the best-trained horse has

'The horses taking fright'. *Julia Holmes*

this first principle of equine salvation at the back of his mind. With many coach horses it was in the forefront. The most innocuous of objects could start off the mechanism, and so accounts of accidents often began — 'The horses taking fright . . .'.

The Yeovil mail leaders shied at an oak tree that had stood harmlessly by the road between Winchester and Andover for centuries. The lurch threw the crew from their seats. Gamble, the coachman, was killed on the spot, the guard bruised. The Kelso coach was broken to pieces when the horses started at the sight of an ass! A young man called Linsell was killed when the leaders of the Leeds–London *Union* 'took fright at a herd of swine' near Skilton; the smack of a pig driver's whip overturned the London–Gloucester *Champion* near Huntley; a small patch of chalk, the *Windsor* near Stanwell. A party of gypsy women in red cloaks caused horses of the London–Ramsgate *Old Telegraph* to dart off 'at a most dreadful rate',

'. . . and had a terrific appearance'

resulting in one passenger being crushed in 'so dreadful a manner as to cause her instant death'.

Paradoxically, horses were potentially most dangerous when at rest — waiting for the off. Again, there was often human failure, as all too often, despite many accidents, coachmen would insist on leaving horses unattended. Impatient, especially the high-mettled animals, they often took off, sometimes encouraged by a noise behind.

Outright abandonment of horses outside inns, common in the early days, while they took a dram, did become less frequent. Then there were misunderstandings. The Manchester–London *Red Rover* had a serious accident in 1836. 'The horsekeeper declares ... he had hold of the leaders, but, understanding that the coachman had mounted the box, he quitted his hold' and the horses started off. The horrified outside passengers began to bale out and, as so often in this situation, sustained serious injury. Soon the horses were 'on the full gallop, and had a terrific appearance .... On arriving at Tillington, ... near Stafford the coach was upset'.[1]

Even when horses were held it was not always enough. As the *Rocket* began to move off from the Gloucester Coffee

'Until it smashed into a cab rank'. *British Library*

House, the Bristol mail horses began to follow, 'notwith-standing the efforts of the man at their heads to prevent them, who . . . finding he could not control them, let go . . . and had a most narrow escape from being run over'. Loose in rush-hour Piccadilly, the Bristol mail whirled off, miraculously avoiding omnibuses, coaches, gigs and waggons, until it smashed into a cab rank.[2]

Perhaps the horses on the Clapham stage can be forgiven their fright when some boys let off firecrackers. Perhaps too the wheeler on the Hereford–Chester mail can be excused the antics which resulted in Mr Watson's servant 'lying in a dangerous state at Church Stretton'. It was stung by a bee. At least, that was the story put out by the proprietors, but it was 'reported all along the road' that the horse had previously worked a post-chaise. Unmanageable there, it had been trans-ferred to the mail.

There were many such horses at work — animals sold into coaching because of 'infirmity of temper'. Others had developed some unsoundness. Many blind horses pulled coaches. Good horses were in short supply and expensive. To cut costs, pro-prietors accepted such animals, the owners only too happy to be rid of them. 'The proprietors are not very particular what kind of horses are used in the night mails,' one coachman complained after being saddled with a blind wheeler and offside leader and having a smash in consequence.[3]

'They were, indeed, often a very queer lot,' remarked one coachman, 'but they had to be driven and were driven.'

The high spirit, not to say viciousness of some gave real meaning to the traditional 'Let 'em go, then, and take care of yourself' to the ostler, following the equally traditional 'All right' from the guard.

Generally described as 'bo-kickers', the worst types of repro-bate horse were known as 'jibbers' and 'kickers'. A 'jib' horse generally refused to start. Coachmen had ways of managing them. Cross cured one by putting him behind two barge horses. Although it threw itself about it had no option but be dragged along, until it rolled into the canal. The horse then gave in. Cross drove him regularly 'and no horse ever went better or quieter'. Edward Corbett found that 'doubling him, that is, making him run his stage double, brought him to his senses in the course of a week or two'.

Bianconi used a pet bull — Flying Dutchman — to cure jibbing horses. One 'fine but dreadfully obstinate jibbing mare' was put in the training break, the bull was attached in front and would 'resolutely put down his horns, and pull the break along, half strangling the mare in her collar as she was dragged along sorely against her will'.

One of Bianconi's horses, Lion — 'a very fine and gigantic black horse' — acted as a sort of trainer. On one occasion 'a sulky, idle beast' was put in beside him. 'Lion seized hold of him by the neck and worried him like a dog worrying a cat and made his legs move along faster.' If willing in harness, it was Lion's only attribute. Before coming into coaches he had killed and partly devoured one man. Fortunately Lion took to one of the horsekeepers and his little granddaughter. With them he was as quiet as a child.

The best drivers came to have a sixth sense about the individuality and temper of their horses. Much depended on positioning. One horse might be disastrous as a wheeler, perfect as a leader. As the coachman stepped down at a 'change' he might laconically address the horsekeeper, 'Put the bay mare near wheel and the stallion up to the cheek.'

Many accidents occurred when a driver took over a team before he mastered their idiosyncracies (and perhaps they, his). The Lincoln–London *Tally-ho* got overturned in 1836 because Berkeley, the regular driver, was unwell and although his place was taken by an experienced coachman the man was unacquainted with the horses and lost control down a hill.

On well managed stages the same horses covered the route day in, day out. They knew the road as well as the coachman, and this saved many an incident from turning into disaster. Time without number a team, bereft of driver, trotted, even galloped on, to arrive quite safely and stop quietly at the next 'change' — not without some palpitations among the passengers. Sometimes insides were never the wiser. When Gamble was killed and the horses galloped off there was only one inside passenger and, 'strange to say, he was not aware of anything amiss until apprised of it by two gentlemen, who succeeded in stopping them, just as they were turning into the George gateway'.[4]

A fresh horse or team could cause difficulties. A new leader in the Norwich–Lowestoft *Pilot* caused the death of Benson

Rathbone, Esq., of Geldestone when it suddenly bolted in 1834. And sometimes unscrupulous proprietors swopped horses about, which was one reason for the Falmouth mail coming to grief on Bodmin Moor in 1839. Apparently it was 'the custom . . . for . . . mail contractors at busy times to use . . . mail horses for all purposes and put such horses in the mail as may at that moment be most convenient . . ., a practice which cannot be too severely reprehended, as the roads in Cornwall are sufficiently dangerous without entailing upon the coachman any increase of difficulty by giving him strange horses unaccustomed to the road, as well as to that kind of work'.

Regular use of the same horses could occasionally cause problems, as when the team of the Hull–Scarborough *Express* 'suddenly turned towards the place where they are accustomed to be watered, and by the swerve occasioned the coach to be overturned'.[5] And once when Captain Haworth was driving the horses were given a longer run than usual. Haworth nursed them past the normal stop successfully, when all at once they shot into the pond — as they usually did when unharnessed from the coach.

For all their pretensions many coachmen were just not up to the job. Rather than they controlling the horses, the 'cattle' so often got control of them. 'The horses becoming unmanageable . . .', following the introductory DREADFUL ACCIDENT, featured all too frequently in newspapers.

First-rate 'artists' were prepared for anything going wrong and when it did, through experience and by keeping a cool head, they could often avert catastrophe. Long experience was not always a safeguard. The coachman of the *Old Telegraph* that came to grief had driven it thirty years. Henry Douglas, considered one of the best 'dragsmen' of his day, lost control and upset the Holyhead mail in 1827 — 'the horses became restive and [then] . . . became wholly ungovernable, and bolted . . .'.[6]

Part of the coachman's control lay in his long whip, which many used all too freely. Miss Weeton on her epic journey was much troubled by the 'change' at Rainhill — 'as the ostlers were fixing fresh horses, one . . . got dreadfully frightened and fell twice . . ., they had some difficulty to rouse it, and then it backed and twisted so . . ., that although there were plenty of men, they had some difficulty to manage it. I expected an overturn.' But the fractious animal was cured on the way — 'the poor horse got well whipped the whole of the stage'.

Many horses had a rough time of it. A coach weighed around eighteen hundred weight, but when loaded they had behind about two and a half tons to pull at speed. And at certain times like Christmas and on 'magazine nights' it was even heavier. When the *Peveril of the Peak* went over near Bedford in 1836 the weight was said to have been three tons — after seven or eight boxes had been taken off and some passengers had alighted in Bedford![7]

Improved roads also increased speeds, which put further strain on horses.

'Do you find . . . increased speed makes much difference in the consumption of horse flesh?' Horne was asked in 1827.

'Considerably,' he replied. 'It wears them out, it kicks all their legs to pieces.'[8]

Many coachmen treated their horses as machines, partly because of pressure to maintain time, but also because they worked so many different animals. There was no opportunity for that bond to grow which often existed between say a carter and the horse he came into daily contact with. The horses of the heavily laden *Duke of Lancaster* were 'wretchedly jaded and altogether unfit for the task imposed upon them' as they laboured through Chorley in Lancashire. 'In every ascent they stopped and backed; in one ascent more precipitous than the rest, they backed, and would not be driven forward. The driver leaped down, and, in the violence of his rage to lash his horses . . . drove the coach into a ditch.'

Omnibus drivers would also use several different pairs in a day. Their burden was even greater because of heavier weights, frequent overloading, constant stopping and starting and the character of the drivers. One horse pulling a Fulham omnibus had a 'raw place under the throat as wide as the collar with blood and pus oozing from the wound'. When John Rogerson complained, James Smith, the driver, laughed and jeered at him. Another, on a Paddington vehicle, had holes worked into the flesh by the collar. These were frequent occurrences. To be fair, although drivers got fined, it was not necessarily their

fault. As James Smith explained more solicitously in court, he
was 'obliged to drive any horses that were assigned to him by
his employer'. Or as another upraided Paddington driver
exclaimed, 'How the hell can I help it?'⁹

It was not that coachmen were necessarily wantonly cruel.
Some were just bad drivers. James Adlam drove the Bath *York
House* from London to Marlborough. 'Adlam made his wheel
horses do all the work . . . and when they were beat made the
leaders pull both the coach and the beaten wheel horses, so
that he got the whole lot well tired before the end . . . , and in
spite of going faster was always late.' Jack Sprawson drove the
coach much better, 'made his horses work level, never seemed
to be going so fast, and yet was always punctual to a minute'.¹⁰

Above all, racing took its toll. Then they were driven so hard
that after three years they were worn out. Some horses died in
harness. One can understand why from the account of a race
between the *Umpire* and *True Briton* Oldham–Leeds coaches
in 1824. They raced all the way and went up and down hills
'both steep and numerous, at full gallop. In going up the hill
which overlooks . . . Huddersfield, the horses of the *True
Briton* were so much exhausted . . . they came to a dead stop
. . . [and] the *Umpire* coach ran rapidly past them. The coachman of the *True Briton* was so irritated . . . he jumped off . . .
and whipped his horses with great severity. At the top . . . he
again mounted . . . and by severe flogging again forced them
into a gallop.'

One outraged citizen wrote to the *Times*: 'The manner in
which horses are driven in stage coaches is disgraceful to the
age in which we live. The knackers' yards may well be
crowded with the shattered remains of what were once — and
might by fair usage, have remained to the last — useful,
unblemished, and happy animals.'¹¹

Short-stage and omnibus horses suffered from racing too.
One housekeeper whose residence overlooked City Road,
Islington, was appalled by the 'furious speed which some of the
omnibus drivers [and Paddington coachmen] indulge in . . . to
gratify a cruel emulation . . . . The pitiful and distressed
condition of many of the horses thus shamefully abused
cannot fail to excite the most painful emotions.'¹²

Horses often came off badly in accidents, as in 1833 when

the cattle of the Leicester mail ran full tilt into the York *Express* near Stamford. The pole of the *Express* penetrated the breast of a mail horse, which, driven forward, dashed its brains out against the coach, shattering footboard and coachman's seat to atoms.

Another unpleasant death occurred in 1828 when the Devonport mail was smashed in London and the horses galloped off 'with great fury . . . but . . . the near leader, a valuable bay mare, rushed against a lamp post with such force, that she broke the spine of her back . . . . The poor beast fell to the ground and plunged with its legs, enduring the most excrutiating agony.' Mr Fagg, the London coachmaster, reckoned, on average, he had two horses killed a week.[13]

One set of horses on the Bristol–Birmingham *Hero* were fortunate in 1821. Stopped on Tewkesbury bridge while the coachman went across to talk to his 'opposite', they suddenly turned round and headed back. Some people tried to stop them, but only alarmed the leaders, who leapt over the bridge. There they remained suspended in harness until they could be hauled back from their perilous position. The *Alert* horses crashed through the cliff railing at Brighton and coach and horses toppled twenty feet, but they 'alighted on their haunches, and strange to say were so little injured, that one of them, later in the day, ran the first stage out . . . in another coach'.[14]

Less fortunate were the Edmonton stage horses in 1829. The offside horse got into a sewer excavation, to hang suspended by the harness. Fortunately, as coach and passengers were being dragged slowly towards the hole, the harness broke. But the animal fell twenty-five feet. The second also tumbled in, and the poor beast fell into an unbricked well, where, after struggling some time, it died. The first horse had landed in the completed sewer and was able to walk along the passage. An earth ramp was built and it was able to climb out. Alas, he was 'much injured'. A wheel horse on the Brighton–London mail got his legs entangled in a wheel on starting off in 1831 'in so singular a manner . . . it was nearly half an hour before it could be extricated, the poor animal . . . groaning most piteously'.[15]

Sometimes such horses could be patched up, but were never quite the same again. John Fair, Brotherton's horsekeeper at Rainhill, told how in April 1826 a driver had come in and explained anxiously 'he had been larking with Sam Scott the night before and begged him to look at the horses and get them bled. The horses were then much exhausted. The near leader, Silvertail, had her jaw bone broken, and the near wheeler was hurt in the chest. He put them out to grass, and afterwards put Silvertail into the *Sovereign* to run a short distance .... On the second journey she broke her leg and [Fair] ... was obliged to shoot her. It was owing to the injury she had before received; two months afterwards the other mare was ill; he tried to bleed her but could get no blood and she died.'[16]

Bianconi paid particular attention to injured horses. His estate was 'overrun with screws of all sorts' which the Italian doctored himself, usually successfully. For leg strains, he put his faith in alum curds in a knitted stocking, and 'many a debilitated animal would be limping about with ... long grey hose ... carefully gartered around his legs'.

Bianconi seemed to take greater interest in his horses than most proprietors, an interest he tried to engender in his work force, insisting their names went on waybills along with passengers'. They were named after their original owners, unless there was some special quality in seller or animal. Miser's late owner always drove a hard bargain. Another, 'a raw-boned brute', was called Rampike.

The Italian knew every horse by name, when and how bought, the cost, and all his faults and peculiarities. His daughter recalled that conversations with Dan Hearn, his general manager, would often go: 'Who says we must take Miss Moll of the Mitchelstown road? She'll do for the Fethard car. Tartar is on his legs again, and will be fit for work next week. Grey Tom is doing well in Sligo, and Tim Healy says he has no trouble at all now with Badger; he goes like a lamb .... Who has Dandy?'

British horses had names too. Miraculous was the only horse rescued from a disastrous fire. The Miller was a violent kicker. There were Holdfast, Anchor, Rocket, Patchwork, Old Crab, Bill the Brewer, Betsy Mare, Old Giles, The Doctor ..., but it is clear they were generally treated less individually than Bianconi's. Stanley Harris remembered some hurried conversations at 'changes', usually about 'cattle', but rarely by name. 'This off-wheeler's a little lame, Jemmy; rest her the up journey tomorrow morning, and put in the old black horse; work the chestnut mare up near leader.'[17]

One might expected horsekeepers to have been more attached to their charges, but again, with much toing and froing, and the numbers involved, there was little chance to build up sympathetic relationships. A kind ostler might be dispirited by treatment meted out to his charges down the road. Daniel Sleigh, a good horsekeeper at Dunstable, used to carry on a *sotto voce* conversation with his horses, wondering 'what they did with them at the other end, and agreeing with himself as to the iniquitous system of taking them . . . into the horsepond, then leaving them to dry whilst Ben Ball — the other horsekeeper — went round to the tap to have half-a-pint of beer . . . . Many of his old friends had fallen victims to this cruel treatment . . .; old Blind Sal . . . caught a chill in the horsepond and died of acute inflammation.'[18]

Ostlers, as a general rule, seemed more like Ben Ball than Daniel Sleigh. Some poor horses suffered dreadfully at the hands of vicious drunkards — men like James Short, one of Edward Sherman's horse keepers at the Bull and Mouth who, in 1825, was 'detected in the act of wantonly and barbariously ill-treating (in a manner too shocking to describe) three valuable mares . . . . One . . . dropped down with the agony . . ., but he flogged her up again and recommenced his barbarities. This animal expired in about a quarter of an hour . . .'. Another died later. 'The sufferings of the poor animals must have been horrid in the extreme.'

John Hall's handiwork came to light when William Lyley inspected his team before setting out for Windsor. Shocked to see the nearside wheeler bleeding from eye and mouth, an eye knocked out, the contents of the eyeball oozing down the animal's cheek, Lyley taxed Hall with misusing the mare. He admitted it, but said she had bitten him.

'You'll hear more of this.'

'I don't care a damn,' retorted Hall. 'I'll kill her.'

It turned out he had struck her with the girth, which he had been tightening when he was bitten. Thomas Peer, the owner, knew Hall was a brute to animals, but as his horses only 'baited' as the Saracen's Head, he could not appoint his own keeper.[19]

Fire was another hazard. Thirty-five coach horses died at the
Bear, Maidenhead, in 1835. 'When the ruins were cleared a
most horrible spectacle was presented in the mutilated
remains of these unfortunate and suffering victims . . ., the
varied positions and writhing forms darkened to cinders,
showed too clearly the dreadful torture undergone . . . . The
fury of the flames was such that the limbs . . . were entirely
destroyed, the blackened carcase in many instances alone
remaining of the powerful frame which just previously was full
of life and vigour.'[20]

By no means all were rejects, 'bo-kickers' or 'old screws'. As
speeds increased, 'swift and high-mettled cattle' were increasingly used. The horses running from London and within a
fifty-mile radius were the best quality — for two reasons. They
had to be fitter because of the less healthy living and working
conditions. London proprietors had to keep an 'army of
reserves', especially where 'working a great quantity of fast
business, or there was competition'. Then, from a publicity
point of view, they had to be 'generally larger and more showy,
than those in the country'. 'Town stagers' — those starting out
from large towns — came to be 'superb animals such as might
be coveted for any nobleman's drag', one enthusiast remembered in 1874. One *Estrafette* horse was 'so fine an animal, as
to have been selected to assist in conveying the high sheriff to
. . . [Coventry] assizes; and they were all well bred and in high
condition'.[21]

A specially fine breed of horse, the Cleveland (from the
Yorkshire district of that name), was bred for coach work, and
some of these 'short-legged quick-stepping cattle' were
extremely valuable, cosseted beasts. Teams were often
matched in colour. Two teams of 'four dapple, smart grays' for
the Blenheim–London coach were said to be worth four
hundred guineas.[22]

The general run were much cheaper. The *average* price of
London horses was said to be between £35 and £45, falling to
about £25 in the provinces and perhaps £23 in northern
counties (roughly the price of London short-stage horses).
Wheelers, usually measuring at least 'fifteen, one', cost a few
pounds more than the lighter horses used as leaders. Blemished,
unsound and vicious horses cost £15 and less. Not that such

Coach horses on the Brighton road

animals, and Cleveland horses, were the only source of horse-flesh. In fact most came from Ireland, and were picked up at large fairs. Horse prices in Ireland were generally lower, but Bianconi admitted paying as much as £40 for a horse, even 'considerably over that'. An average price was perhaps £15–£18, although 'sometimes we get a good horse for £5 and I sometimes pay £30 for a bad one'.[23]

Horses past their prime sometimes went on to provincial routes, then ended their career on slow night coaches. It is said that the word 'nightmare' originated from their terrible existence.

Despite the high consumption of horseflesh some, when well managed, did survive to be 'useful, unblemished and happy animals'. (Even some blemished horses survived. Old Blind Sal worked the same ground thirteen years and Lion pulled cars to 'a great age', although 'never losing his ungovernable temper'.) A bay leader worked the Taunton–London *North Devon* daily, without exception, for thirteen years between Somerton and Wincanton. In 1837, aged seven-

Horses on the slow night coach

teen, it was in 'as fresh and . . . as good working condition as any horse of the set'. 'This fact,' concluded the *Taunton Courier*, 'attests the advantage of careful driving and is very creditable to Stevens . . . to whose conduct the North Devon coach has been intrusted so long.' Really good drivers, given decent horses, could and did bring in the team almost as fresh as when it set out, on time and without accident.[24]

These horses were exceptional. Captain Haworth reckoned horses loved coach work, apart from a few 'underbred vulgar screws which can take delight in nothing'. In reality, for most, it was no fun to be a coach horse.

9

IT WAS INDEED MISERY

Additional dangers, difficulties and discomforts came from a source no one could do much about — the weather. It was not unknown for coaches to be whirled over by wind in exposed areas. In 1838 the York mail went over on Blackstone Edge. In northern Scotland the mail overturned at Dalwhinnie Inn through 'an impetuous gale of wind'. Farther south, the Edinburgh–London mail driver was plucked off at Abbotsford. The guard dropped off to get at the horses, but, the crew's weight lifted, equilibrium was lost and coach and horses were swept into an adjoining field, rolling over several times. Crews regularly had to be strapped to the seats when passing over the fells.

Wind increased the burden on the cattle. In the West Country, as the Devonport mail approached Deptford Inn in the teeth of a gale, 'on reaching nearly the top of Castle Hill ... the horses could not face it, and they became unmanageable and stopt, when the violence of the gale actually drove the mail backwards, and the horses, almost worn out, were dragged after it for several yards, until the coach was stopt, at the side of the road, and instantly blown over'.[1]

In 1822 western Britain was struck by a hurricane which did great damage, including blowing over the Holyhead–Shrewsbury mail twice between Tyney Maes and Capel Curig. Roads were strewn with uprooted trees, bringing further dangers. The Birmingham–Bristol mail turned a corner near Kempsey to be faced by a tree of immense size 'which, but for the adroitness of the coachman (Garland) in pulling up his horses ... might have proved fatal'.[2]

Moses Nobbs once had his coach blown over, but whenever it was windy after that he took 'the precaution of opening both doors and tying them back, so the wind might pass through'. With storms came floods. In 1829 a bridge in Cheshire gave way during floods, precipitating the Birmingham–Liverpool mail into the swollen Weaver. Coachman Bell fell among the thrashing horses and, although injured, managed to reach the bank. Moreton, the guard, was swept away until he caught hold of a tree, hanging for an hour before a rope was thrown and he was rescued, 'almost as much dead as alive'. One 'thin active young man' managed to squeeze through the coach window, but others were 'too lusty to pass' and perished. The coach was swept away with three horses which also drowned.[3]

The bravery of a servant saved passengers on the Milford mail eighteen months later. A quick thaw after heavy snow caused flooding in South Wales. Eight miles out of Carmarthen a stream had overflowed the road. The horses began to swim, got entangled in the harness and drowned. The coach fortunately remained upright, but stood marooned in roaring water.

The guard blew his horn but at 2 a.m., in an isolated spot no one came. The night was pitch black; the water rising. The two inside passengers grew increasingly alarmed as it reached the seats. The servant of Sir Richard Phillips, MP for Haverfordwest, stripped and courageously plunged into the maelstrom. After much exertion he reached solid ground, made Halfway House and roused the landlord. They sought assistance of the Towey fishermen, who, after great difficulty, managed to save crew and passengers, the water by now almost up to their chins.[4]

Even on balmy summer days all was not perfect. 'The roads laid on McAdam's plan, are better for carriages and easier for draught horses,' Miss Weeton admitted, 'but for human beings in dry weather, are almost beyond endurance; they are one continuous cloud of dust, blinding to the eyes, filling the nostrils, going down the mouth and throat by quantities to suffocation and completely ruinous to all decent clothing . . . . If Mr McAdam could lay the dust as well as the roads, he would be a clever fellow.'

Winter brought fog, ice and snow. One of the worst accidents in fog occurred in 1838 when the Exeter–London *Defiance* hit a dense patch seventeen miles east of Exeter and 'notwith-standing the greatest care . . . [by] coachman (Charles Bevan), . . . a steady sober man, the coach got on a bank . . . and was instantly overturned' and everyone thrown from their seats. The driver was killed instantly, a passenger died soon after, the guard was severely injured and two passengers broke legs.

To hurry in such conditions could be fatal. In 1822 a Woolwich coach, 'driving at a quick rate . . . ran against a heavy country cart loaded with dung. The stage was instantly upset and the people on the roof were pitched with great violence against an empty coal waggon passing by', injuring them all. In town when conditions got bad coaches were pre-ceded by two link boys on horseback and often a man ran along holding the leaders' heads.

In icy conditions horses were prone to fall, and great caution was needed, but one mail team got so frightened south of Nairn they broke into a gallop and took the coach over a fifteen-foot bank.[5]

A London fog. *British Library Newspaper Library*

If Mrs Weeton found conditions 'piercingly cold' in May one can appreciate what it must have been like in wet, freezing, winter weather. Even an enthusiast like Reynardson in *Down the Road* had not quite forgotten his sufferings 'on a journey from six a.m. to six p.m. outside . . . amid the snow and rain till coats, hats and the very flesh were wetted through to the bone. It was indeed misery!'

Stanley Harris remembered having 'rain running off the brim of my hat for some twelve or thirteen hours consecutively', and the greatest annoyance was to have a woman behind with an umbrella. 'First . . . she would poke it against the back of your hat and nearly shove it off; then, . . . catch hold of the brim with one of the points and almost pull it off . . .; and lastly, . . . shove it just below your hat so adroitly as to send a little stream down the back of your neck before you were aware of what was coming.'[6]

Coach proprietors could hardly be accused of mollycoddling outside passengers, and rarely issued protective clothing such as aprons, nor was any attempt made to keep the seating dry.

'Not so exposed': Bianconi's car. *British Library*

In contrast, Bianconi gave great thought to *his* passengers' comfort, providing them with 'dry and comfortable horsehair cushions and aprons, which no coach establishments do to their outside passengers generally'. The cushions rested on a slatted rack which prevented the wet soaking into them and in wet weather were changed after two stages. Also, on cars, passengers were only about two feet from the ground and were less exposed.

People died through exposure, including the outside passenger — 'a poor man' — found stiff as a board on the Dover mail at the Elephant and Castle in January 1838. Charles Cahill remembered how, after eighteen hours from Perth in deepest winter, he and his fellow passengers arrived at the Union Hotel, Inverness, unable to move. 'The hospitable landlord, Mr Cockburn . . . at once ordered his men to get us down and carry us to the back kitchen, where there was a large fire, the floor being strewn with straw, on which they placed us, in a row in front of the fire to thaw.'

They lay there some time before limbs began to loosen. A glass of the best 'Old Scotch', kept specially for the purpose, completed the cure. 'But the effect it had upon me for some weeks after was anything but pleasant,' he recalled — whether referring to the cold or the whisky is unclear.[7]

Not that passengers on the *Auxiliary* London–Exeter mail would have complained of cold in January 1821 when it was discovered to be well on fire near Crewkerne. Friction in badly lubricated wheels caused such fires, which were not infrequent.[8]

Crews, although better equipped to face rigours of weather, suffered too. Thomas Turner, driver of the Halifax and Pontefract mail, had been 'so much frozen . . . during the late frost, as to render it necessary to procure assistance to lift him from his box seat, on its arrival at the Griffin Inn, Halifax . . .'. One guard got so benumbed that he dropped from his seat near Newark and remained stranded until a following coach picked him up.[9]

Surprisingly, snow seems to have caused no great impediment in England for most of the coaching age. In mountainous regions of Wales and Scotland it was a different story. 'The journeys in Scotland during the winter season were no luxury,'

Cahill recalled. On one cold, snowy night, going from Inverness to Perth, coach and horses plunged into a huge drift beneath which a torrent roared. The coach was helplessly wedged. 'We wrapped ourselves in big coats and rugs and resignedly composed ourselves in a bed of snow. In about ten minutes we became exceedingly warm and we all slept soundly.

'We arose with the dawn and having refreshed ourselves with a draught of good highland dew we began . . . to dig out the coach. We completed everything satisfactorily and were soon again on our journey to Perth, where we arrived six hours late.'

Passengers on the Edinburgh–Glasgow mail, stranded by a snowstorm near Kirleston in March 1827, were less fortunate. The guard went off with the mailbags and the driver returned to Edinburgh 'with a view, it was understood, to get fresh horses. The passengers . . . were compelled to wait in the coach . . . in a very solitary part of the road . . . through a dark and stormy night, with a broken pane of glass, through which the wind blew bitterly cold'.

The driver returned with two horses, collected a few articles from the coach and jestingly asked the passengers what they meant to do. It became clear he was leaving them to shift for themselves. He was 'persuaded at length to aid one who was faint and unable to struggle through the snow . . .': the others were left to extricate themselves as best they could.[10]

Snow was not *generally* disruptive in England — with the exception of the Christmas fall of 1836, which more than made up for previous mild winters. There had been nothing like it since 1806. It began on Saturday, Christmas Eve, and continued several days. Worse, north winds created prodigious 'wreaths' and as soon as passages were cut through, snow was driven back, choking up the roads again.[11]

London was effectively cut off from the provinces for several days. For over a week the network was in chaos, with coaches bogged down, everything out of place. 'The stables of the coach proprietors in and around London,' reported the *Times* of 28 December, 'are completely exhausted of cattle owing to the non-arrivals from the country.' On the road horses were reported 'dead beat' from struggling through the snow. It was

'Plunged into a huge drift'

pitiable to see them 'sobbing and sweating, the wet pouring in streams from their sides'.

The Devonport mail passed through Amesbury, then 'The leaders dropped down but rose again; the near wheel horse fell and could not be got up. The coachman went back ... and returned with a pair of post horses. The only good they could do was drawing the wheel horse out ...; they could not put him on his legs. The post boy was sent back, and returned with four more post horses, and four fine waggon horses .... With these combined assistances the mail after being delayed three hours was got loose by daylight. Leaving their own jaded horses behind, they travelled onward with the six post horses across the downs .... The near wheel horse left behind could not be got on his feet for two hours afterwards.'

The Sheffield *Hope*, which left Mansfield with eight horses

'Leaving their own jaded horses behind ...' The Devonport mail goes on over Salisbury Plain with six fresh post horses, December 1836. *British Library*

and arrived in Nottingham (several days later) with ten, was a week on the road to London. St Albans was full of coaches that could neither get up nor down. Between Slough and Salt Hill sixteen mails were in the same predicament. Near Bristol a hundred passengers congregated at two small public houses, where only three beds could be made up. Between Mansfield and Nottingham four coaches got stuck in a remote spot. A labourer's cottage was the only place of shelter, and there the sixteen passengers sought refuge. There was only one chamber above and precious little to eat. For several days they lived exclusively on a pig the cottagers killed. The snow around the cottage lay nine feet deep.

Passengers on the mail from Exeter were luckier. They were five times buried in the snow, but in one place a kind-hearted farmer, after lending his team and men to release the mail, insisted they refresh themselves at his farm before pressing on. He placed before them cold fowls and bacon, with good home-brewed ale, and added a glass of brandy and water each as a 'digester'.

Some enjoyed the experience. Guard Goodwin remembered 'the "lark" at Dunchurch, when all the up night coaches were detained two days .... We had a very nice school of guards and coachmen, I can assure you. My party was located at the Dun Cow, the opposition, or Red Rover party, at the Green Man .... The first evening we had a pleasant dancing party, Mr Brick, the worthy host, having invited a few of his friends. On the following, I turned wandering minstrel, taking with me a chosen few. We patronised a few farmhouses on the Rugby road. Another pleasant evening, and off to London the next morning.'[12]

Others had less happy memories. When the Boston mail stuck fast the seven passengers were obliged to get down and lend assistance behind. One passenger on the Brighton *Times* 'was so fatigued by his exertions in helping to get the coach along, that when they arrived at Patcham he was taken very ill and was obliged to be put to bed'. Perhaps the sole passenger on the London–Newcastle coach would have done better pushing. On arrival he was 'so numbed with cold that he could not move a limb and was obliged to be removed from the coach and placed in bed ...'.

It was especially hard for coach crews. They came out of that desperate week with great credit. Passengers of the Manchester–London *Bruce*, for instance, were in despair, but were constantly encouraged by the 'intrepidity and astonishing exertions of the guard'.

Not all passengers were as appreciative. John Bayzand got with great difficulty as far as Gore Hill, heading for Southampton, already an hour late. Snow came down ever faster, so that one side of the coach was completely covered. The inside passenger put out his head and asked Bayzand if he knew where he was driving to.

'Well, sir,' he replied, 'to tell you the truth I don't.'

'Oh, indeed! What a fellow you must be to be trusted to risk the lives of Her Majesty's subjects.'

'Perhaps you'll be kind enough to get out and show me the right road, for I don't know it, and I drove along it a great many times, and with perfect safety.'

In something of a temper the inside got outside and fell into about seven feet of snow, crying out 'most lustily'.

Bayzand and two outside passengers retrieved him and put him back inside. Just then a farmhand rode up to tell Bayzand the road ahead was completely blocked, whereupon the coachman 'with great danger and difficulty' turned the *Oxonian* round. They made it back to Oxford, but with snow coming down faster than ever another trial was not made for several days.

Of course stagecoach guards, like Goodwin, could abandon the journey and stay with passengers until conditions improved. Many stagecoaches, like the *Oxonian*, turned back and others never set out. But the mails had to go through, and if the coach could not be got on guards must press forward with the bags, and by and large, through appalling difficulties, they ensured it was done.

The Birmingham via Banbury mail of Sunday night got nearly to Aylesbury when 'the horses ran into a drift of snow, which caused the off leader to fall, and he got under the pole. The off leading rein, two traces, and a splinter bar were broken.' After making all right they made another effort, but it was no use, as snow got deeper farther north they went. It was blowing a hurricane of driven small snow. The horses shook with the cold.

The crew took the horses off and led them and the passengers back to a farmhouse. Then the guard hoisted the mailbags on his back and set out to walk into the teeth of the storm to Aylesbury. There he saw Mr Hearn's foreman, who procured men. They went back, dug the coach out and made a road across some fields. A team of waggon horses dragged them into Aylesbury Monday noon.

They were soon joined by the up guard, with four horses, who had not only abandoned the coach some seventy miles from London but a post-chaise as well south of Bicester. *He* pressed on to London, eventually arriving near midnight on Monday, after much deviation from the road, 'in a most distressing state of exhaustion'. The down guard obtained fresh saddle horses and set out north, leaving coach and passengers at the George, in Aylesbury. There was a strong wind and snow kept drifting all day. He arrived at Bicester at ten o'clock Monday night.

Conditions continued to deteriorate, but the guard was anxious to press on. No one could be persuaded to risk their horses, though, and the guard was compelled to stay all night.

The guard presses on with the mailbags

Next morning he started for Banbury on horseback and found the road deep in snow, as much as eight feet in places, but he struggled on to Birmingham.

The Gloucester–Brighton mail, too, was caught in the first full might of the storm and had to be abandoned at Southwick, but the crew pressed on with the bags in a cart along the beach, where, overcome by intense cold, they could have perished but for rescue by the coastguard. They finally arrived at Brighton half dead from cold.

A following Gloucester–Brighton mail got firmly stuck on Salisbury Plain. It took eighteen carthorses to drag it across fields, preceded by men cutting hedges and rails in its path. The coach eventually reached Salisbury, where it was left. The guard went on — for forty-eight hours without rest, and some guards struggled through for even longer.

Guards were so long on the road a shortage built up. Relief guards were all out too, and some mails had to be 'intrusted to clerks and other confidential persons' hastily sworn in. When guards did finally get in, often after most harrowing journeys, they must needs soon get out again. Neal arrived in Hull with the London mail on Monday night, after abandoning the coach near Wortleby on Sunday night, and was off back to London again on Tuesday morning with two days' mail on horseback.

By Thursday conditions were easing. The wind had dropped, the snow stopped and passages cut through drifts no longer filled in again, but travel was still difficult and unnerving. Griffin, coachman of the Norwich–Newmarket mail, was nearly six hours in going twelve miles and was once completely buried. 'The snow in many places, where it has been dug through . . . was in many cases higher than his head as he sat upon the coach box.' The guard of a Gloucester–London mail reported, 'the impending snow hung over so frightfully that he was momentarily expecting that the rolling of the coach wheels would bring down an avalanche upon them'.

Coachmen played their part too, struggling on through appalling conditions, but true glory went to James Carter, on Sherman's Portsmouth–London *Star of Brunswick*. 'The only roads that have been clear throughout the storm,' reported the *Times*, 'are the Portsmouth and the Poole.' This was due not to greater clemency on the Portsmouth road but to the initiative of James Carter.

Around Hindhead snow lay as deep as elsewhere and had 'drifted into fantastic wreaths and huge mounds by the fierce breath of [the] . . . wild December gale'. At the steep hill by the Seven Thorns Inn, Liphook, coach after coach came to a dead stop. 'The tired wearied exhausted cattle refused to struggle through the snow mountains any longer. Guards, coachmen, passengers and labourers attacked those masses of spotless white with spade and shovel but to no purpose.' Passengers stamped their feet and blew on their hands. Men shouted, grumbled and swore, while women shivered and waited. It began to look as if the night would be spent in these Arctic surroundings, and they were almost resigned to it, when . . . along came James Carter on the yellow-bodied *Star*. 'He made very little to do about the matter, but whipping up his

'He made very little to-do about the matter.' James Carter on the Portsmouth road

The end of a hard day and a hard week. *Julia Holmes*

horses, he charged the snow drifts boldly and resolutely, and with much swaying from side to side opened a path for himself and the rest,' and thus was the Portsmouth road kept open.[13]

Not that there was anything new about guards doing their duty. Stories are legion of men who struggled on from whatever catastrophe to see the mail through, but efforts during that difficult Christmas week were so obviously heroic and seen on a huge scale to be so that, coming as they did on the eve of the sudden end of the coaching era, they left a fine memory of the industry at its best, which lingered on and pushed unpleasant aspects to the back of people's minds.

Perhaps this is only fair. Although the contemporary coaching industry was never seen in the rosy hue it later came to be bathed in, we must be careful, in making a more realistic appraisal, not to go too far.

10

PECULIAR TO THEMSELVES

It is strange there should have been such opposing views of coach people. It can partly be explained by the obvious fact that all sorts of individuals worked in the coaching industry, good and bad, and some good on some days; bad on others. There is no doubt, too, that later writers glossed over faults and failings through romantic nostalgia. But there was a rapid change in personnel after about 1820, not least in coachmen's character. Drunkenness, for example, declined. Too many coachmen of the old school still drank, and drank too much. Their indiscretions kept the old public image alive. But there were fewer of them as they retired, were killed or injured through their own inebriation, or were sacked because of the growing weight of public concern. A new wave of recruits was coming forward to replace them, men of more temperate habits, who, because of the strange nature of the calling, became 'a class of men peculiar to themselves'.

By 1834, a disinterested observer like Edwin Chadwick reckoned, 'many of those vehicles are now conducted by men greatly advanced in intelligence and respectability, and I was recently informed ... they now find it conducive to their general health and power of enduring the weather, to pursue a more abstinent course, and ... they more frequently take tea, coffee, or milk and avoid the general or frequent use of a strong stimulant when on duty'.[1]

This impression was confirmed in 1837. 'No set of men have been so greatly improved ... as stage coachmen; as individuals they are now not more remarkable for civility and steadiness than they are as a body for sobriety; tea, or more generally coffee, having almost superseded the use of spirituous liquors among them.'[2]

Whatmough, on the *Peveril of the Peak*, was one of the new respectable coachmen, but he made it clear that there were still some of the old guard around in recalling: 'Other drivers, when they felt cold, used to drink brandy and water, and then shortly would want another glass, but I never drank anything but water.'[3]

Of course, there had always been good steady sober drivers, like John Barker of the *Regent*, an 'old fat coachman . . ., a good, kind old man . . ., a good though not at all a swell coachman . . . as safe as the bank . . . who had driven from Stamford to Huntingdon pretty nearly every day but Sunday for more than twenty years'. Into his careful hands the young Reynardson was entrusted on journeys to school in the early 1820s. There were others like him, but they had been a minority. The

'Entrusted on journeys to [and from] school'. *British Library Newspaper Library*

change was wrought swiftly. By 1832 Peter Mountain felt 'the majority of them certainly do conduct themselves very well . . . I believe . . . coachmen . . . are very well behaved men.'[4]

Bianconi, too, succeeded in building up a team of respectable, sober drivers. 'Many of them were well-to-do in the world,' his daughter remembered, 'and showed by their general appearance that their families were honest and respectable.' Many were the sons of prospering yeomen.

Some coachmen may have been gay dogs and enjoyed their virile image, bantering with barmaids, but in truth there was little of the 'larking and kissing' supposedly widespread. On the main coach routes there was 'no time for such pleasantries . . . . The fast coaches rarely took more than a minute-and-a-half . . . to effect the change of horses; the coachman very rarely left his box and the guard had barely time to attend to his parcels and get his time bill inspected.'

The mail guard had become as a rule 'a taciturn and calculating kind of biped, sternly desirous, of course, of doing his important duty, resplendent in the uniform of a Queen's officer, frequently passing among the uninitiated as a clever man, from the now well-worn habit of holding his tongue because he had nothing to say; and while never above receiving a tip, rigidly decorous in the matter of "liquoring up" at the wayside inn'. He was 'generally fully conscious of his own dignity and inclined to "stand upon it" at the slightest provocation'.[5] Many were probably boring old sticks. Stagecoach guards also became generally more responsible, while remaining more lively and cheerful.

Bookkeepers, although some may have been sharp or offhand, and perhaps pushed employers' interests before clients', were generally held in high esteem in the community. The bookkeeper at the Angel, Oxford, was Old William Jacobs — 'a highly respectable, intelligent man', according to Bayzand. At the Star was William Scott, 'a well-informed man'. Samuel Cave was another dependable sort. He had been clerk and bookeeper at the Saracen's Head, Snow Hill, for fifty-four years. He never complained of illness and was invariably in jocular humour, still at work at seventy-five. John Jones, at a Brighton coach office, was so highly thought of his passengers raised a subscription when he had a financial misfortune.[6]

Perhaps improvement filtered down into ancillary staff too. There *were* honest, respectable, sober porters and horse keepers — like Daniel Sleigh. He never went to no 'public 'ouses, nor yet no churches'. He *was* rather odd. He 'kep' 'isself to isself' and rarely conversed with anybody but ' "his 'osses," ' with whom, between the h-i-ss-e-s which accompanied his every action, he carried on a *sotto voce* conversation'. Apart from six weeks in the 'horsepital' following a kick from a horse, he had never been beyond the smithy for eleven years. His personal appearance was 'not engaging — high cheekbones, small gray sunken eyes, a large mouth and long wiry neck, with broad shoulders, a little curved by *anno domini*'. He always wore the same clothes, a long plush vest, once blue, a pair of drab trousers 'well veneered with blacking and harness paste', black leather leggings meeting thin ankle boots. A 'no-coloured string which had once been a necktie' and a catskin cap completed his wardrobe. Before moving to the Sugar Loaf, Dunstable, Sleigh had been with Mrs Nelson in London for thirty-nine years.[7]

How was it possible to recruit the large number of additional people needed in the 1820s and 1830s, and at the same time recruit a better type of person? Increasingly, crews were drawn from more elevated positions in life, not a few being aristocrats or gentry, and not all had necessarily fallen upon hard times. They tended to be attracted first to more fashionable routes like the Brighton, Oxford and Bath roads. As the *Times* noted in 1833, 'Well-born coachmen prevail on the road. A gentleman connected with the first families in Wales, and whose father long represented his native country in Parliament, horsed and drove one side of the ground . . . with Mr Stevenson [a Cambridge University graduate] and Mr Charles Jones, brother of Sir Thomas Tyrwhit Jones, has now a coach on the Brighton road, called the *Pearl*, which he both horses and drives himself'.

The Welsh gentleman was in fact Mr Sackville Gwynne, son of Colonel Gwynne, who had estates in Carmarthenshire. Following a property dispute he had quarrelled with his father and become a professional coachman.

There was at least one clergyman — 'Parson' Dennis — who exchanged his Berkshire vicarage for the box of the Bath *White Hart*.[8]

The trend spread from these fashionable routes. The older, rougher style of coachman remained more in evidence farther from London and main routes, but from Birmingham there were professional gentleman coachmen like Tom Bainton on the London mail, Will Wilder on the *Potteries* coach, Mr Flack on the *Patent Tally-ho,* and Mr Marsh 'avec son grand air' on the Birmingham–London *Crown Prince.*

Many 'gentlemen' drivers were military officers who forsook their profession for the road. Also out of Birmingham were Captains Probyn and Warbrick on the Cheltenham road, Captains Pead and Douglas on the Derby road.[9] Captain Douglas drove the Birmingham and Sheffield mail and was 'a quiet nice coachman who after a long stage of sixteen miles to Lichfield brought his team in fresh'. He had seen service in the Peninsular war. Out of Manchester there was Whatmough, who had held a commission in the Scots Greys.

A fair number were university-educated. Peter Mountain in 1832 employed 'men brought up at college'. A guard on the Carlisle mail was known as 'The Collegian' for this reason. A *Peveril* guard was one of the Manchester Labreys, a rich Quaker tea-dealing family.[10] Hugh Black, who came into coaching in 1824 as guard to the Leeds–London *Rockingham,* formerly kept the White Swan, Leeds.[11]

It is difficult to find an area from which crews were not recruited. One coachman had been a publisher; one guard a clown in a circus. Heyden, driving an Oxford stage, was son of a market gardener in Thame. Many, like Ben Holmes, whose grandfather was a Birmingham horse dealer, had had connections with horses.[12] Moses Nobbs's father was a Norwich coachbuilder and he was being brought up in the business, but the road called and he began as a mail guard in 1836. A prospective Post Office guard had to be recommended to the Postmaster General by a Member of Parliament, and Moses got the job in return for a favour his father had done an MP.

What brought such men on to the coaches? Peter Mountain explained simply, 'they are fond of driving'. Whatmough told Slugg he became fond of horses and driving and took up the occupation simply from the love of it. Increased speeds required greater skills, giving greater status to the art of driving.

Many recruits were of humbler origin. Colonel Moberley,

Secretary to the Post Office in 1838, claimed, 'We take a man from the plough and make him a guard.'[13] Men came up from the ranks. A Manchester–London *Telegraph* guard had been a musician in the Grenadier Guards. 'Matty' Marsh had served as a private with the Fourteenth at Waterloo and drove for many years from Maidstone to London. A few had been private coachmen — domestic servants. Some horsekeepers rose to the bench. Sometimes proprietors were prepared to give horse-keepers who showed talent a chance to take a stage occasionally with the regular driver and they advanced from there, usually doing a spell as guard first. Often they got their chance when the regular driver was unavailable at short notice, like the Balcombe horsekeeper who smartly filled the breach when Pickett got kicked. He took the *Item* safely on to London.[14] Bianconi made a point of taking his drivers 'from the lowest grade of the establishment; they are progressively advanced according to their respective merits, as opportunity offers'. Some porters got their chance too, first as spare, then as regular guards and sometimes on to the box. A fair number of post boys, like Dick Vickers, Tom Holtby, William Hall and John Edwards, changed from saddle to bench. In fact this seems to have been a common way to the top — stable boy, horse-keeper, post boy, coachman.

Richard Blight, born at Totnes in 1797, began his career in the Seven Stars stables aged seven. He showed considerable aptitude and was soon promoted to riding leaders of the lumbering coaches. A spell as post boy followed, and at seven-teen he was established coachman of the *Sovereign Traveller*, eventually becoming regular coachman of the crack *Quick-silver* mail.[15]

Bill Tolley began as an odd boy at the Hen and Chickens, Birmingham. In later years he used to pucker up his face at recollections of thirty or forty pairs of boots, forty or fifty dozen knives and steel forks, to be cleaned before breakfast.

Tolley's bright looks and general intelligence soon relieved him from drudgery. On proving he could drive a pair he was appointed Mrs Waddell's coachman on a six weeks' carriage tour. Good living, comfortable lodgings and 5s a day generated ambition, and Tolley determined to work his way to the box seat of a first-class coach. He got to be guard on the Shrewsbury and on easy stages gave the coachman 'a bit of a rest', thus learning how to manage a four-in-hand. After twelve months he boldly asked Mr Waddell for the Oxford coach, proved his ability and at the age of twenty-two reached his goal — one of the foremost positions in his profession. Later promoted to a Liverpool coach, the *Erin-go-bragh*, he remained there until the Grand Junction Railway opened.

For such men as Tolley and Bright, and many more, mingling with 'gentlemen' professionals and frequent contact and conversation with 'class' passengers led to a 'softening and refining [of] their rougher natures'. Tolley became 'a splendid specimen of the florid school of coachmen . . . his face mellow with rosy colour, bronzed by the weather, merry with buoyant humour, and glowing with the tokens of abundant vitality . . . and if fortunate to secure the seat by his side, his jovial voice, his contagious spirit of fun, and his inexhaustable store of droll story . . . made you sorry when your journey came to an end'.[16]

Coaching was the passport to a life of wealth and status for many of humble origins. Harry Horton became a crack guard on the *Patent Tally-ho* and a finished performer on the key bugle. His aged parents used to watch him go through 'with a look of proud satisfaction that their son Harry was acting as guard'.[17]

Above all, men came into coaching because the money was good. On the face of it coachmen were poorly paid. Their weekly wage was between 10*s* and 16*s*, roughly the sum earned by an agricultural labourer. In fact they were extremely prosperous, since it was accepted by both proprietors and passengers that most of their earnings would come from tips. The process of extracting the tip was known as 'shelling' or 'kicking', where coachman or guard would approach passengers, hand outstretched: 'I am leaving you now, sir.' The standard tip was between 2*s* and 2*s* 6*d* per fifty miles, and £300 was an often quoted average annual income from tips, although the value of 'drives' differed considerably. But one which did not bring in a pound a day was not thought much of. Some were worth double. Jack Willan, who drove the *Times* from London to Brighton and back, was said to make £700 a year, but as Lord Algernon St Maur added, 'a man who drives one hundred miles, every day, in all weathers, deserves to be well paid'.[18]

In Ireland too 'perquisites' were often 'very considerable'. It was Bianconi's standing joke that the better a driver the more he reduced his wages — because on good routes he more than made up for reductions with increased tips. Some famous coachman only received 2*s* 6*d* a week in wages, but on night mails and unfrequented roads the pay went up to 15*s* — in itself no mean sum in the Ireland of the 1820s and 30*s*.

Then there was money to be made from 'shouldering' and many coachmen horsed one or two stages themselves, for which they got a cut of profits.

In addition, services carried out by coachmen merited reward — in kind if not in money. On the parcels Ben Holmes rushed around to the *Times* it was clearly marked that if delivered by three, the bearer was to receive a sovereign; if by three-fifteen, 15*s*, and so on. George Young, coachman (and guard) on the Leeds *Union*, added no small amount to his regular pay through transacting business and carrying huge sums of money for people. He was a keen sportsman, and from his knowledge of the turf he carried on a sideline as a book-maker. John Everitt, of the crack Shrewsbury *Wonder*, another sporting coachman, well up in secrets of racing, cock fights, prize fights and other sporting events, supposedly acquired a large fortune through knowledge picked up on the road.[19]

Some were showered with gifts by admiring gentry — whips, boots, greatcoats, hats. One squire promised Cross, the coach-man from Littlehampton to London, 'George, the next time I win the Derby I'll give you a team of four greys for your coach.' By the time he *did* win the Derby, Cross had left coaching but received a letter: 'George, you don't want the greys now, but I send you a cheque for £100 to do what you like with.' And many a 'douceur to guard and coachman ... made things all right' when amateur coachmen wanted to take over the ribbons.[20]

Guards too were poorly paid on the face of it. Post Office guards received 10*s* 6*d* a week, a uniform and a pension. Ordinary coach guards were paid rather more. Chaplin paid between 10*s* 6*d* and 15*s*, plus uniform. Again passengers were 'the principal means of support', and substantial it could be. A place on the *Quicksilver* was said to be worth £160 to £180 per annum in 1832, and many were worth more. Again a figure of £300 per annum has been mentioned.[21] Guards expected at least half a crown from every passenger per hundred miles. If less, 'the guard looks at him very hard'. A journey from London to Manchester would set the traveller back at least 5s in guards' fees on top of the 5s for the five drivers.

Guards did favours for people, too, for which they were certainly rewarded, and if Bill Bayzand's experience is any guide many stagecoach guards were in business for themselves, carrying little extras regularly. Bayzand used to bring a sack of watercress up from Witney to London, bought for a sovereign, sold for two. He also dealt in fish, eggs, poultry and meat, including saddles of Welsh mutton.

Such dealings were quite acceptable to the *Mazeppa* proprietors, or at least to the London bookkeeper, Mr Southam, who quite openly arranged a deal between Bayzand and a West End poulterer starved of turkeys, by which the guard made a substantial profit.

William Chaplin admitted that 'in the coaches there is occasionally perhaps a little private trading of their own', but, he added firmly, 'with the mails that could not be done' — or so he thought!

Post Office guards were more circumspect, being liable to the sack if caught carrying their own goods. But they still did it. An Exeter mail guard carried live calves up in the boot, since veal was 'cheap in Dorchester and dear in London, and there's a crown to be got out of that calf, only the London butchers like them alive'.

He nearly came unstuck when Chaplin got in. The guard became nervous — 'now that Billy is inside perhaps I'd better cut its throat, as if he hears it "bah!" I might get into trouble'. Fortunately Billy fell asleep, the animal stayed quiet and was swiftly hidden in the mail cart at Piccadilly. Richard Butler, a Dover mail guard, was caught smuggling a large quantity of lace in the hind boot.[22]

Then there were the bankers' parcels sewn into a guard's coat. The bank paid carriage and gave a sum to the guard. John Baker received 6s 8d for the parcel he carried, and it was often done regularly, usually by mail guards. Guards received gifts too. Jack Goodwin could boast 'nine bugles and cornopeans . . . presented me while stage coach guard'.[23]

Certain expenses had to be offset against these substantial incomes. Coachmen were expected to pay 1s a week to their horsekeepers. They were often fined if late and sometimes had to pay for damage caused by negligence — Scott, of the *Champion*, had to pay £28 4s for injuring Brotherton's horses. Guards, too, had to find about 5s a week for the mail coach porter at the Post Office and other incidentals. They were sometimes made to pay for lost or damaged goods, and when first taken on paid a deposit for this purpose. And some gilt was rubbed off mail guards' gingerbread in 1838. They did get a pay rise, from £27 7s 6d a year to between £70 and £130, depending on length of service — a substantial sum, but they seemed unhappy. A journalist went studying them at work in the Post Office Yard found: 'Somehow or other these officers have lost much of the spriteliness of their original character: they seem to be dejectedly brooding over the innovation made upon privileges long vested . . ., to wit, the right they once enjoyed to soliciting compensation in the shape of fees from passengers. We strongly suspect that to these hardy servants of the public a fixed salary is a fixed injustice.'[24]

Of course, by then guards had other matters to brood over, but during coaching's heyday crews were men of substance in the community who, by today's standards, would equate more with air crews than bus crews.

Bianconi's agents (bookkeepers) were well paid, too — from £52 to £72 a year according to the station. At the smallest, agents were part-time — generally shopkeepers — receiving a commission of five per cent. Salaries of British bookkeepers are difficult to find and no doubt varied. Thomas Capps, bookkeeper to Stevenson's illustrious *Brighton Age*, earned five guineas a month.[25]

Earnings of other ancillary workers are equally hard to come by, but the indications are they were above average for the type of work. For instance, amorous Charles Fashnact, the boy of fourteen who was an *assistant* to delivery porters at the Swan with two Necks, was paid 12s a week in 1826. Porters also did well out of tips.

Horsekeepers too were by no means badly paid. A statement

of account for several Lancashire coaches in 1830 lists '87 men as ostlers etc. at £1 per week'.[26] Then there was the 1s weekly from one or several coachmen and perhaps board as well. Thus horsekeepers, like many others in growth industries during the industrial revolution, did well.

Ostlers' wages before the French wars were abysmally low. George White, twenty-one years old in 1784, who looked after John Stoney's stage horses at the Cross Keys, Stony Stratford, started off at 12s a year plus board, although by 1794 he was earning 18s. Richard Sims, thirty years old in 1794, who worked variously at the George and Talbot, the White Lion and the Bell Inn, Melton Mowbray, between 1789 and 1793, was never paid more than three guineas a year (and presumably board). Wages rose during the French wars, and some of these advances were held when prices fell afterwards, but John Smallby was still only earning 10s a week without board as ostler to John Scohey at Stilton in 1818 when he was twenty-five.[27]

There were ostlers and ostlers — some in charge of a large number of horses and others perhaps little more than cleaners and sweepers, but the message is clear: many men could rise to earn at least £1 a week by 1830, which was no mean sum. Equally, in Ireland, Bianconi's stable 'helpers', as they were called, were paid from 10s to 15s.

Wages of coachbuilders are symptomatic of how men prospered in the growing industry. John Wade, a London coach maker, complained in 1835, 'we are paying considerably more now that we were in the time of war; the men we used to pay a guinea and a half a week to, we are now paying them two guineas; and everything was so much dearer then than it is now'. Some men on piecework were earning as much as £6 a week.[28]

It is difficult to establish what inn staff were paid, although indications are that, relatively, they did as well as others in the industry. It is equally difficult to establish from whence these ancillary workers came. Innkeepers were often sons of innkeepers. John Fowler's father had been proprietor of the White Hart before him; his grandfather, of the Crown, Amersham. Some were former coachmen who invested in an inn as they aged. Thomas Pye, who drove the Edinburgh mail between

Doncaster and Stamford, took the New Angel Inn, Doncaster, continuing to drive. Joe Scott, 'a very stout, good-looking' coachman, married the daughter of the landlord of the Golden Lion, Catterick, and in turn became landlord.

A fair number had been butlers in domestic service, like Willie Carver of the New Inn, Easingwold, in Yorkshire; Harker of the York Tavern, York, later known as 'Harker's Hotel', had been butler to a Colonel Croft. The landlord of the Anchor Inn, Liphook, had been a servant to the Duke of Clarence, later King William IV, a beneficial connection. Many were drawn 'from a superior class', Tom Bradley remembered, and John Fowler claimed, 'they were generally men of superior education and manners, from their constant association with the leading nobility, clergy and magistracy'.[29]

Some servants, too, had previously been in domestic service. As for the rest, who knows? Your typical London porter, according to Tristram, betrayed, 'I fear, a Celtic origin' when he spoke and no doubt there were many Irishmen at work throughout the business, not least with horses.

Of the four ostlers recorded at Northampton, three had first-worked on the land. Coach proprietors and innkeepers usually had farms, and men often found their way into horsekeeping after service on their farm. This happened to John Smallby, who first found employment on John Scohey's farm at Thorn-haugh in Huntingdonshire before looking after his horses. Benjamin Kite was born at Devizes about 1738. At fifteen he enlisted in the Artillery, until disabled and discharged. He returned to Devizes and worked at the Bear.[30]

If the experience of these eighteenth-century men is any guide to later recruits, many were drawn from the land and had led something of an itinerant life. Perhaps after the French wars there were many discharged soldiers, like Benjamin Kite, who, having worked with horses in the army, found work with them after 1815.

11

DIFFERENT TEMPERS
TO PLEASE

What did the work involve? Coachmen, of course, drove the coach and we have seen some of the difficulties, not least from perverse cattle and vagaries of weather. Many day coaches ran without guards, and the coachman had to fulfil the function as well: attending to passengers — 'the different tempers to please inside and outside the coach' — waybill, parcels, loading and unloading, skid pan . . . . A guard was supposedly senior partner, keeping the driver from drink, recklessness and up to time. He had to get to the horses' heads when stopped, or jump off to encourage them on hills. Post Office guards also had to attend to the mail.

Coachmen's hours were relatively short. They benefited from improved technology in travelling the same distances as in earlier days but in less time. Between seven and eight hours was the average spent on the box of a 'long coach', but some drove as little as five. Charles Ward drove the *Quicksilver* sixty miles a night; Bill Harbridge the Manchester mail a hundred. Bianconi's drivers went twenty to thirty miles out and the same back, but at a slower pace.[1]

These short hours did involve intense, tiring concentration and were often awkward and anti-social, with one night in two frequently spent in lodgings. Mary Harris kept a lodging house for coach crews in Birmingham and explained how Robert Platt 'came home at seven o'clock on the morning of the 30th; he was driving all the night long; he had his breakfast and went to bed . . .; he got up about three, had his dinner and went out; he returned again and went to bed . . .; he got up at half-past nine and had some coffee with . . . Weedon [the *Crown Prince* guard, also lodging there]; he left my house at a quarter past ten to go to the *Standard* coach . . .'.[2]

Ned Mountain drove the Exeter *Defiance* ten hours through the night for years. He became unwell, and when the doctor cross-examined him it emerged that he always took a pipe and a glass at eight o'clock every morning. The doctor expressed astonishment he was still alive after drinking in the morning. 'It may be morning to you,' retorted Ned, 'but it's my bedtime and I can't lay off.'

Social life could be difficult in other ways. Many coachmen never married, hence perhaps their gigolo image. As Bob Pointer explained, 'When a man is always going backwards and forwards between two points, what is the use of a wife? A coachman could never be much more than half married. Now, if the law — in the case of coachmen — allowed two wives . . . he could then have the tea-things set out at both ends'. At least one coachman adopted this solution. Bill Bowers, Black Will, driving between London and Oxford, 'had a snug establishment at both ends'.[3]

When on the fast Manchester–London coach, Whatmough arranged with another driver that each should drive ten hours to Derby and back, on alternate days, so they might avoid lodging there and sleep at home each night, being compensated for the long hours by a day off.[4] Other drivers made similar arrangements and where possible would take a coach out and bring another back the same day. But the schedules did not always allow such arrangements. These split days (or nights) could be tedious if there was a long wait between driving stints. Thomas Cross, on the *Crown Prince*, started from London at 5 a.m. and drove to Redbourne. He then had to wait from eight-thirty a.m. until 6.00 p.m. for the up coach from Birmingham, arriving back in London about nine-thirty. 'At first I felt this vacant time as a great inconvenience, which, however, I presently found means to alleviate by indulging in my fondness for books; and frequently, on a fine day, I would saunter about the lanes and fields with one in my hand.' He became acquainted with the local gentry and at dinner with one he over-indulged and had his incident with the *Crown Prince*. Waiting around no doubt encouraged other coachmen to pass time with a glass.

The guard's job was physically more arduous, since, whereas coachmen changed, guards stayed aboard throughout, which often meant twenty-four hours without rest. (In later days Post Office guards were limited to 100 miles.) Guards were more active. Robert Oxenham, Exeter *Subscription* guard in 1822, explained that in the 180 miles to London a guard would be up and down thirty to forty times.[5]

They had to be physically fit, especially as they might be called upon for some exceptional exertion. During one particularly bad winter Moses Nobbs rode and tramped through terrible weather for fifty consecutive hours seeing the mail through. They had to be quite muscular, shifting heavy luggage and even heavy passengers. Slugg remembered the Lord Nelson's guard was 'one of the tallest, handsomest and best built men I ever saw .... I recollect seeing him ... lift a corpulent lady down from the top ... with the same ease with which I should lift a child from off a table.'

After twenty-four hours on rolling coaches, often in adverse weather, guards must have welcomed journey's end. They were then compensated with days off. Manchester guards, for instance, used to leave on Monday, rest on Tuesday in London, set out again on Wednesday to arrive back on Thursday, rest on Friday and start again on Saturday.

Climatic conditions were sometimes extreme; at the best of times never very warm, often wet. But coachmen were usually well protected. Two moderately thick coats were found to give more warmth and keep out wet better than one thick one, which became insufferably heavy after hours of rain. An ample upper neckcloth kept wet out; body heat in. 'Coachmen's cuffs' stopped draughts up sleeves. Over the second coat went an ample waterproof cape with sleeves, and an apron over the legs. Coachmen also had dry woollen gloves and whips in reserve. There were other dodges. Old night coachmen often had bands of hay or straw twisted round their legs — not considered quite the thing among the new wave of 'dragsmen'.

Guards wrapped up well too, but less comprehensively so as not to impede movement too much. And they could use their hands to hold an umbrella, hunch under a waterproof or turn from driving rain. Bill Bayzand seemed to manage well enough, even during one particularly wet October. 'I could keep myself quite dry,' he remembered, 'with one exception of my seat getting wet.' Dampness in the behind concentrated his mind and he suddenly thought to try a large gridiron.

'So when I reached Oxford, I purchased one . . ., cut off the handle, strapped the gridiron on the seat, with my cushion on the top. I could defy the rain, as I could see it run underneath in a regular stream; so with a Mackintosh apron, and my cape over, I could keep myself perfectly dry. And ever after, coachmen, and guards especially, adopted it from the Bolt-in-Tun and Bull-and-Mouth yards, and called it the Mazeppa Patent'. No one ever thought to give passengers' seats the same treatment.

In any incident the guard had to sort things out. When Garland pulled up the Birmingham–Bristol mail just short of the huge tree in 1822 it was the guard, Pope, who 'instantly commenced severing with his axe the huge limbs and heads of the tree' and supervised the removal of the barrier when help arrived.

Guards carried tools in case of breakdown and were expected to execute repairs. They were men of initiative. Once near Ross the *Mazeppa*'s pole broke.

'Fowles, do you see that hurdle?' Bayzand pointed to a nearby sheepfold.

'Yes.'

'Fetch it.'

The driver dutifully obeyed. 'I took it to pieces, nailed the long parts on each side of the pole, bound a strong cord round tight as I could, then some wedges; drove them well home . . . and put a chain on each side from the roller-bolt to the cock of the pole.'

The coach was delayed only twenty minutes, and the jury pole survived to London and back to Oxford.

Another duty was, with porters' assistance, to load 'as much luggage [as] I could stack on the roof (and as we were allowed to carry by Act of Parliament) — securely made fast with four wide leather straps, covered and made waterproof with tarpaulin: the front and hind boots full, the iron behind full and covered with waterproof; with cradle slung on the hind axletree full of fish — and [on] every available part of the coach, packages of all kinds hanging on the lamp irons and ladies band boxes with light articles, strapped on the seat irons . . . . It was surprising to see the packages stowed on the ground, and wonder where they could all be put in so short a space of time by the guard.'

Loading up: guard supervises porter

For all that some coachmen and guards could be tetchy and supercilious, and all too often gave the treatment they thought accorded with the size of likely tip, there is no doubt most considered it their duty to entertain and safeguard the interests of their charges. Some were particularly concerned. Of Hugh Black, guard to the Leeds–London *Rockingham*, it was said to be 'no unusual thing for persons about to set out for the metropolis to defer their journey . . . for the purpose of placing himself and luggage under his care'.[6]

Having made much of the ill conduct of guards like Blake and Stringer, we must mention everyday kindnesses to passengers from men like Hugh Black. Many a time, if it came on to rain, would a guard usher an outside woman inside. Bill Bayzand was a kindly man. Two penniless sailors, robbed in Gloucester, were on the *Mazeppa* 'without grub or bub or a shot in the locker', so at Cheltenham he bought them a loaf and a quart of shrimps, at Dowdeswell Hill fish and bread and at Northleach some rum. In London he paid for a cab, gave them two and sixpence each, and sent them off to the docks. 'We'll never forget you, mate.'

Some time later the porter at Gloucester asked if he could decipher the directions on a parcel. He could make out Ga—d, M—pha, C—h and suddenly realised it was for him. Inside were a thousand cigars — 'the very best I ever smoked' — and a small scrap of grimy paper thanking him for his kindness.

Richard Blight, the West Country coachman, was 'respected by all classes. To the really poor his heart and pocket were always open.' And there could, of course, be some awkward customers. One can understand some of the tetchiness. The Shrewsbury *Wonder*'s driver was given two nasty-tempered leaders to manage, requiring all his attention, when a talkative old gentleman began pestering him. 'Whose house is this?' Whose park is that?' 'What spire to the left?' 'What tall column to the right?' To all these questions the coachman answered curtly, 'I don't know.' The man lost his temper, and petulantly inquired, 'What *do* you know?'

'I know,' was the rejoinder, 'how to drive the *Wonder*.'

One Methodist minister kept insisting on thrusting religious tracts at a coachman *in extremis* with a runaway coach until he was finally driven to mutter, 'Oh dear! oh dear! Whatever can I do with your papers; however can you be a-giving me papers now; no skid on, pole-chain gone, and never a bit of gravel . . . to run a wheel on. I don't see as we shan't be over yet; so if you happens to know anything short, sir, now's your time.'[7]

One can understand, too, the difficulties of London drivers in crowded, competitive City streets, with no shortage of over-righteous, military and other gentlemen prepared to hand out a 'good threshing' at the slightest provocation. One got into a fearful temper over the 'unworthy conduct' of an omnibus conductor who forgot to tell a woman where to get off, carrying her a little too far. He protested he had been too busy, but the matter could not end there, meriting a letter to the *Times*![8]

There had always been decent, steady men among London coach and bus crews. One woman complaining in 1830 was 'equally desirous to do justice to others who conduct their business with much regularity and corresponding civility'. Some at least of the animal-like conduct in London was due to the fierce competition and lack of organisation. Crews were under considerable pressure from proprietors. Even later in the century William Parragreen — Cast Iron Billy — was sacked for refusing to race younger drivers. Nevertheless, legislation and the formation of increasing numbers of associations *did* bring improvement from the late 1830s. Omnibuses started at short and regular intervals and in general came to be 'conducted by men of sober and respectable character', and there was greater supervision. In 1837 Nimrod visited the Elephant and Castle, an important and once chaotic staging post for coaches and omnibuses heading south. 'I found evident improvement in the conduct, the language and the general deportment of all . . . and it must be admitted that improvement was much wanted.'[9]

Another bugbear was the common informer — 'a sneaky sort of rascal, who, nevertheless, performed some service for the good of the community'. With no effective police force, and with accidents increasing from overloading, an Act of 1788 had laid down the numbers to be carried and decreed that half the penalty should go to the informer. Increasingly complex legislation followed — about luggage, lettering, licence plates, etc.,

Cast Iron Billy (*left*), *c.* 1870, sacked for refusing to race. *London Transport Museum*

and it became possible for men to make a living out of informing.

One can understand that they were not popular with coach-men, but, in fairness, informers, who had the law at their finger-tips, harried them for petty, obscure infringements. As one remarked, 'he had nothing to do with the intention of the legislative, he depended upon the construction of the wording of the Act'. Nor were they above inventing offences. William Trip was found guilty of perjury in 1822 after alleging the Exeter *Subscription* had been overloaded. Joseph Wise and William Jefferson got six months' imprisonment in 1824 for falsely accusing Thomas Greenfield of overloading his Henley stage. When Wise discovered that several witnesses would be called against him he offered to drop the charge . . . for a sovereign.[10]

The most notorious was Byers, who set himself up as a master informer in 1825. The richest pickings were in London, but these men also went on roving commissions to provincial towns to capitalise on lax law enforcement. In November 1825 Byers was in Bath, where he laid thirty-four informations in two weeks, bringing in fines of nearly £500. Visits to Bristol, then Oxford, were marked by a string of prosecutions. He was on the road again in 1827, to Brighton in the summer, followed by a spell in Hampshire in August. Resentment built up. The public generally saw informers as sneaky, low fellows — 'worthies' and 'supposed gentlemen' as one newspaper described them with heavy sarcasm. One magistrate told Byers he had 'no particular leaning towards him'. In Winchester he was paraded in effigy on a gibbet, but, unable to lay hands on him, a large crowd began to pelt his assistant, Rawlins, with eggs and filth. They followed him into a house, poured boiling water over him and beat him savagely.

In an earlier case at Kingston one London informer, Charles Hutchin, had been pelted with muck, rotten eggs and stones until he 'resembled a pillar of mud'. He jumped into the Thames to escape, but the mob dragged him out, tore off his clothes, ducked him until almost lifeless, then shaved off his whiskers.

Byers always seemed to escape through the back door on such occasions. He was still at work in October 1832, when he won a typically nitpicking case, but in that year an Act changed the rules. The whole penalty was now to go to the Crown and, although the court had discretion to give part to the informer, the rich pickings were over.[11]

The bookkeeper's job was a responsible one. He was effectively in charge of coaching operations from his particular office. He paid out wages to guards, coachmen, porters and horsekeepers, and kept them up to their work, kept accounts, received bookings and packets, saw passengers and parcels aboard, bore responsibility for valuables, answered complaints and chased up unpaid fares. He was often also responsible for the stable accounts.

At more important inns some work was delegated to clerks, but overall responsibility remained his. At less important stopping places he often had to combine several functions. At small roadside inns the landlord usually acted as his own bookkeeper.

In smaller establishments he could have his hands full. Thomas Paine, bookkeeper at Maidstone coach office, had a bad morning in 1824. He had received a parcel containing £13,000. The following morning he brought it down and put it on his desk. By five-fifteen the coach, still being got ready, was a quarter of an hour late. He was called out into the dark inn yard to remove a quantity of hops which some people were arguing were in the way. Back in a couple of minutes, he had to go out again to arrange the passengers' accommodation. When he returned the parcel was gone.[12]

In Ireland 'agents' played the key role occupied by bookkeepers in Britain. Like them they were in charge of the complexities of the waybills handed to each driver every morning, showing the names of the driver, the horses and the towns *en route*, with the hour of arrival or departure at each. On subsequent pages passengers' names were entered, showing boarding point, destination and fare paid; the total sum was filled in at the bottom. Goods were entered in like fashion. Each addition *en route* was accompanied by each agent's initials. These details had to be copied into day books and sent to head office every three days, as were the waybills. Each agent had also to furnish monthly accounts of receipts and expenditure. At head office all was cross-checked meticulously

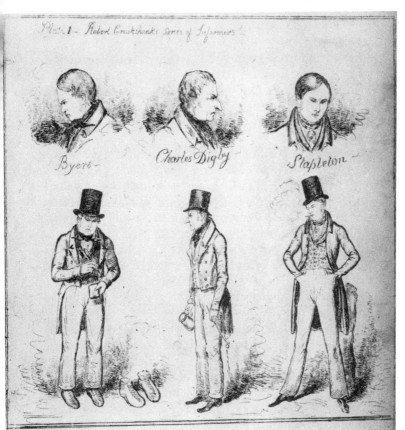

Plate 1 - Robert Cruikshanks Series of Informers

Byers -   Charles Digby   Stapleton

BYERS the notorious Informer & his assistants.

Byers (principal Informer) age, about 35 years- 5 feet 3 inches in height - thick set - florid complexion - two or three spots over the left eye brow - dirty flaxen hair - grey eyes, having a down cast look - forehead extremely prominent - bumble feet usually with high low boots laced to the toes - somewhat shuffling in his walk - dress rather slovenly -

Charles Digby (assistant to the notorious Byers) aged about 50 5 feet 3 inches high — a thin man having a long hatchet shape pointed nose — a small wart or pimple on the right side- between the nostril & cheek - grey eyes - grey hair and whiskers - a red hot weather beaten countenance, in combination with a sly down cast cunning look —

Stapleton (deputy Informer to Byers) age 35 - about 5 feet 7 inches high round face- florid complexion - a furrow between the eye brows - grey eyes - ty down cast look - light hair generally combed off to the right - rather dandified in appearance - his hands commonly in his trowser pockets- & flashey in his manners —

Published by Robt Cruikshank, & to be had at all the Licensed Victuallers in Soane and Camden New Town — Entered at Stationers Hall

Informers — 'sneaky, low fellows'. *British Library*

by Bianconi and his secretary, and woe betide the agent whose accounts did not balance. Rigid allowances of feed were laid down for each horse. One of Bianconi's most trusted agents was once short of twenty-eight barrels of oats, and although there was no suggestion of dishonesty, he had to make up the deficiency.

An unusual feature of Bianconi's establishment was the female agents — as many as twenty out of about a hundred and thirty. They were generally wives or daughters of deceased agents. In Britain female bookkeepers were rare (although there were numerous women innkeepers, usually carrying on after a husband's death). There *was* fair Miss Newbury, who kept the Plymouth office. She tempted coachmen with 'little peculiarly refreshing stimulants' but when she 'at last discovered that her charms were not properly appreciated among people living in a higher circle' she married the head boots of the Royal Hotel.[13]

Bookkeepers, too, obviously worked awkward hours — exactly how long is uncertain. In larger establishments much routine work could be delegated to clerks; in smaller ones sometimes the porter might do it, so the bookkeeper could get some rest. For instance, when an elm box was brought to a coach office in Coventry at 5 a.m. a young porter booked it in. The bookkeeper did not come on duty until later — and, being suspicious, ordered the box to be opened and found 'the body of a young female in a state of preservation'.[14]

In Ireland the agent had to be at his post at the arrival and departure of every car and coach, and the same was probably true of many British bookkeepers. This meant they often had to be on hand at night, the most irksome part of the job.

It is a mystery how long porters worked, but again they must have been early out of bed and busy late into the night. The young porter who received the elm box at five in the morning was still at work twelve hours later when the body snatcher — 'a low-sized young man' — called to see if it had gone off. They worked under the bookkeeper's direction, loading and unloading, carrying passengers' luggage. Ticket porters had the regular job of delivering goods, but there were also jobbing porters — casuals who hung around inns hoping for a rush of business or an urgent dispatch — men like Thomas Caves, an unemployed omnibus conductor, who plied about the Blue Posts, Tottenham Court Road. Such men could make immediate delivery, whereas there was delay if a parcel was booked through the office, but there was less control over them if anything went wrong.[15]

Hours worked by horsekeepers were surprisingly short, if Peter Mountain's evidence to the Select Committee on the Observance of the Sabbath is accurate and typical.

'How many hours a day are the horsekeepers engaged?' he was asked.

'Seven or eight or nine hours, those that have twenty horses a day; it depends upon the number . . . they have to look after.'

These were probably ostlers in London stables. It was unusual to look after so many horses. Outside the large stables they had fewer horses to attend to but probably worked longer hours. In Ireland night horsekeepers worked from six to six. 'All the helpers had hard work; they usually had each five horses to clean and feed, to harness and unharness'.

Horsekeeping was a responsible position. Apart from feeding, and doctoring the animals, cleaning them and their harness, they had to be got ready for the coach. Harness was supposed to be checked by the driver, but often there was no time. A mistake could have drastic consequences.

Corbett confirmed that horsekeepers were generally a 'rough lot', but it was a rough job. 'They were frequently expected to attend to eight horses, four out and four in, every day, or to take charge of six, with eight out and eight in, during the course of the day. But . . . worse . . . they constantly had vicious horses to attend to, . . . dangerous to approach in the stall . . . . It struck me as not very enviable to be left, in the middle of the dark night, to look single-handed after four dirty horses, and one of them a "savage."'

Francis Crease, an experienced ostler at the Golden Cross, was kicked in the groin and abdomen by the Guildford mare and died. William Taylor, at the Kings Head, Great Surrey Street, was cleaning a 'fidgety' horse when it lashed out and broke one of his ribs, piercing his heart.[16]

We have seen how many coachmen perished or were injured in their calling, although we have perhaps not highlighted the most common and terrible calamity that could befall them —

'And one of them a "savage"'

being jerked off among the horses, to be kicked and trampled to death, like Henry Strivens of the Tunbridge Wells–Brighton coach. Brydone, of the Manchester–Carlisle mail, caught up in the reins, was dragged along behind his runaway horses.[17]

It was an extremely fortunate guard who was never in an upset. Peter Banks, 'having seen so many accidents of that kind, and being aware of the danger, disentangled his legs from the seat, and was ready to jump . . .' when the Holyhead mail overturned. Many guards were killed and injured. There were less obvious dangers. A London–Boston mail guard, putting on his greatcoat, 'was thrown out of his dicky by a sudden jerk of the coach'. Hugh Black was killed when flung from the *Rockingham* as it turned sharply into the yard of the Gold Lion, Leeds.[18] The skid pan was a fruitful source of danger. Bill Bayzand had a near escape when the skid chain broke and whipped through the air. 'Had I been one moment longer I must have been killed.'

Another time he really was injured. Guards could usually put the skid on (and even take it off) without stopping the coach. But the road was greasy, and he slipped and found 'my right foot skidding the fore-wheel, my left foot hold of the roller-bolt .... Bray pulled up as quickly as possible, and I was released, with the bone of my great toe broken.'

He was taken to the Staple Inn, Witney, but 'The poor woman that acted as nurse, without looking at the directions on the bottle the doctor sent, gave me the lotion to drink, and I thought I was poisoned.' He did gradually recover from both disabilities but was off work for a month.

He also had a lucky escape once when loading: 'the luggage strap broke and pitched me on my head — fortunately into a case of hats. I played the deuce with the contents, but ... it saved my head .... Ever after, if I saw the slightest fault in a strap, I cut it in two.' A surprising number came a cropper through this. Friend, coachman of the Hastings coach, dislocated his collar bone, and Tom Peck of the Birmingham–London *Eclipse* actually died in Coventry when the strap broke and he crashed his head on the pavement. This incident wrought two casualties. Peck and Bob Hassall, the driver, were close friends. He saw Tom fall and instantly fainted. When he revived he was a hopeless lunatic.[19]

Porters had similar mishaps. George Taylor, at the Brighton *Accommodation* office, was severely injured when 'the back of his head came with great force against the kerbstone' when a strap gave way. George Amsink, at the Swan with two Necks, had his leg fractured when a heavy package fell on it. Another porter was bringing a drink to a lady inside the *Alert* at Birmingham when a fellow porter on the roof let slip a large trunk on to his neck. When the Bristol mail careered off from Gloucester Coffee House in 1836 a porter called David, who had been on top fixing the luggage, was flung off.[20]

After damning the character of London porters it is fair to point out that not all were of Robert Eson's stamp. There was the young porter named Jones at the Green Man and Still who, when the high-spirited cattle took fright and bolted, seeing the danger to passengers, sprang forward, and seized the leaders. He was thrown down and trampled on.

Similarly, horsekeepers may have been a wicked lot, but more than a few were injured and killed trying to prevent horses taking off, men like Edward Mitchell, who hung on grimly to the *Times* horses after they had bolted through Brighton. He finally lost hold, fell under the wheels and had to have a leg amputated.

There was Edward Harvey, aged forty-two, a Greenwich coachman, who 'met his death in endeavouring to avoid doing injury to the woman who was crossing the road', and Langford, who although 'mangled in a frightful manner ... was most anxious to render assistance to the others and could scarcely be prevented from an attempt at personal exertion'. And there was the guard whose drunken driver fell from his box, the horses bolting. He scrambled over the top, let himself down between the wheelers, edged along the pole and recovered the reins, to save mail and passengers.[21]

Whatever its image, there were some good brave men in the coaching industry.

12

FOR THE SAKE OF
PUTTING THEM ON

Often revered in later times, proprietors were more usually seen as villains then. In public eyes they waxed wealthy at others' expense and were none too particular about their safety. 'Is Mr Brown content to revel in the wealth he has accumulated from public conveyances, at the expense of the loss of life and limb . . .?' railed the *Taunton Courier* when the *North Devon* had again overturned. After an accident on the Birmingham *Eclipse* an enraged correspondent had some advice for Mr Waterhouse, 'who is so large a gainer by the use, and one might say abuse, of these public carriages . . .'.

Some proprietors were decidedly off hand. When the Hereford–Chester mail went over in 1828 the passengers remonstrated with the owner 'on the impropriety of putting dangerous horses to a public conveyance, [but he] behaved with the greatest insolence, saying, if they did not like it they might leave the coach, as there were other passengers to take their places . . .'.[1]

Proprietors came in all shapes and sizes and in large numbers. Horses were the key to coaching. The simple idea of short stages gave unparalleled speed but also generated complexity and great expense. The number of horses demanded and consumed was enormous. An 1829 statement for thirty-three Lancashire coaches lists:

Harness for 709 horses at £4 per year each	£2,836
Iron and labour to blacksmiths for 709 horses at £3 per year	2,127
87 men as ostlers, etc., at £1 per week each	4,524
Rent of stable and coach offices	1,418
Consumption of horses, say 709 at £15 each to be renewed every three years	3,545

Hay and corn for 709 horses at 15s per week each	27,651
Straw at 2s 6d per week	4,615
Deduct value of manure, which is calculated at the price of straw	4,615
	£42,101

Turnpike tolls added a further £8,005, and a staggering £14,496 was paid in various taxes, making a grand total of £64,602. This excluded wages to coachmen and guards or any allowance for coach purchase or hire (proprietors hiring London coaches paid about 3d per double mile).[2] Some huge sums were paid in taxes. Benjamin Horne paid £26,717 a year in mileage duty alone in 1836, before an assessed tax of £1 5s on each coachman and guard, plus £5 licence fee for each coach annually.[3]

Few men alone could afford to horse a 'long' coach for the whole of its route, and it would have been difficult for one man to keep a watchful eye over it. Bianconi managed it in Ireland by being often on the go himself, but also through a system of three agents or inspectors, each paid £120 a year. Bianconi had additional reports from spies. There were two full-time spies who operated until their 'cover was blown'. Then there were occasional spies, often schoolmasters on holiday, happy enough to travel for nothing. They reported on everything — horses, the behaviour of personnel ('anything calculated to offend the public was always punished'), punctuality, and any discrepancy between actual passengers and those on the way-bill was immediately investigated.

In Britain a system of capital-cost saving and extended control evolved. It is true the industry came to be dominated by relatively few men — the London coach proprietors (owning vast numbers of horses and the great London inns), and some substantial proprietors in provincial cities and towns. In their hands lay much of the organisation. But the industry was maintained by 'small' men, often fair capitalists in non-coaching fields, but really in coaching as a sideline.

A proprietor or contractor was simply the supplier of horses, the coach usually being hired from specialist contractors (in many ways also partners in the venture). London and provincial proprietors would 'horse' a coach a few stages out of London or a major town, but then 'country' proprietors took over for one or two stages each. Similarly 'cross' coaches (i.e. those that did not touch London) might be horsed by 'small' men organised by such as Richard Costar from Oxford. Thus no 'spies' were needed in Britain because each proprietor kept a close eye on his own stages (although the Post Office had inspectors).

'Country' proprietors were an interesting group, and in some ways the importance of proprietors like Horne and Chaplin has been exaggerated to their detriment. 'There is a general notion that our contracts are to be settled with such persons as Mr Waterhouse and Mr Sherman in London,' said Charles Johnson, Superintendent of Mail Coaches in 1827, 'but that is not the case; all the parties that work in these contracts consider themselves entitled to give their vote and their opinion quite as freely as the London contractors.'[4]

Not surprisingly there were somtimes disagreements. It was rarely that they went as far as the proprietors of a London–Exeter coach in 1824. One, Loaring, landlord of Heathfield Arms, Yarcombe, had dealings with a rival coach. The others gave him notice, which he refused to accept. He continued to horse the coach as usual, halting it forcibly outside his inn and attaching his own cattle. The driver was obliged to dismount and the innkeeper's servant was put up.

The dispute became increasingly furious. Waggons blocked the road, attempts were made to by-pass the inn, traces were cut and 'pugilistic encounters' became ever more frequent, in one of which another proprietor lost part of his thumb. The row went on for at least a fortnight. The final outcome is not clear, but the public had been so frightened off that business was 'for want of harmony and co-operation . . . , in a fair way of utter destruction'.[5]

Who were these country proprietors? The Post Office, when starting a new mail, looked first to people already running a coach. If they could not be tempted innkeepers, stable-keepers, farmers — 'anybody at all engaged in the horse line' — were approached, Johnson explained.

Occasionally a coach was organised and horsed by tradesmen. The fishmongers of Bristol were behind a Bristol–Exeter coach in 1821. A group of Huddersfield businessmen put on the Manchester–Leeds *Commercial Union* in the same year. Some unusual characters were attracted into coaching, including two silversmiths in York. Richard Colls, an assistant surgeon at Worcester in 1825, came to horse a London coach nine miles and the *Independent* fourteen miles, in partnership with Thomas Becket — but only for a few weeks. Becket went bankrupt and Colls did a spell in jail. A dapper little doctor, George Alderson, took over the Angel at Ferrybridge along with its coaching.[6] Mr Perkins, a bookmaker, horsed the London *Sovereign* out of Worthing. He failed too. Whitbread, the brewer, horsed the Bedford *Times* out of London with 'some rare trotters'.[7] At least two coaches were started in a fit of pique. The Marquess of Worcester put on two coaches in opposition to Sam Goodman, driver/proprietor of the Brighton *Times*, because the 'surly cross-grained fellow' had refused the keen amateur a drive. The new venture was done with great flair — too much flair, since it was involved in several disastrous and expensive smashes.

The groom of Richard Walker, a rich Sussex squire, inadvertently sold his fine horse Robin instead of Rollin. The squire was 'terribly vexed' and determined to have him back from the purchaser, George Cross, the Littlehampton coach proprietor, but was refused.

'What,' shouted the squire in a towering rage. 'Can't have my horse back again! Well then, — me if I don't ruin you!'

Walker started a competing coach, and a lavish affair it was, but it was he who was ruined and had to sell his mansion and beautiful park. Cross drove on.[8]

Coaching was far from being the licence to print money outsiders thought and required considerable expertise, not least in judging horseflesh.

There were also many coachmen who horsed one or two stages, and sometimes, like Chaplin, they became substantial proprietors. But innkeepers like Loaring formed the greatest proportion of these small men. They went into coaching to bring custom to their inns — at first so people would stay the night, and later, as speeds increased and overnight stops diminished, so they would eat there.

For this reason London proprietors had great difficulty finding partners to work mails within twenty-five to sixty miles of London, 'for there are no refreshments . . . coming at

that time of the night . . .'. They all started from London at
8 p.m. In fact the mails became increasingly unremunerative
and difficult to horse as the fast *day* coaches increased. The
Post Office was obliged to keep upping the rates, but profits
remained scant. John Hart, a Birmingham proprietor, told an
1832 Lords committee 'I worked three of His Majesty's Mails
that did not pay me'. It was fairly universal and got worse. The
'Mails unfortunately do not flourish except into very populous
towns,' Chaplin claimed in 1835.[9]

Even stagecoaches, which could carry more passengers,
became unprofitable as costs rose and competition increased.
Spin-off profits to innkeepers from dining disappeared for
many, as Christopher Kemplay, a settling agent for several
northern coaches, made clear: 'it was the case in former times,
but now the great rapidity with which the coaches are hurried
along . . . had greatly diminished the advantages . . . coaches
could produce to an inn.' He could 'safely and conscientiously
say' coach proprietors' business had been unremunerative for
some years.[10]

The public *thought* proprietors were making large sums at
their expense. One company established the Leeds–Newcastle
Joint Stock in 1834 because 'they fancied there was an
unwholesome system carried on by the innkeepers who were
hitherto chief coach proprietors'. After eighteen months they
were forced to give up after losing thousands of pounds. Joint-
stock enterprise was rare in coaching and, where it existed,
usually unsuccessful. A General Stage Coach Company was
formed in 1825. The prospectus listed the existing evils — fees,
imposition at inns, etc. — which would be eliminated. It
began service between Brighton and London, but died within a
year.[11]

Perhaps people were misled by the obvious wealth of
Chaplin, Horne and Sherman, even of Costar and Brotherton
(whom Chaplin describes as 'an exceedingly opulent man' in
1827).[12] But they had real advantages over country proprietors.
They horsed the most lucrative ground. They owned the great
inns that *were* profitable. Visitors up to town *did* base themselves at the inn of the coachmaster in whose coach they came.
And it was only in theory proprietors down the line were equal
partners. Accounts were settled (monthly) on an equal mileage

basis after deductions for taxes, coach hire, etc., but the share-out was less equal than appeared.

'As an old coach proprietor, I must perforce recount a few of the grievances which we country proprietors loved to air,' Fowler wrote. 'The London firms had many great advantages. Every coach that left any booking office was charged over £1 per month for booking passengers, and as many hundred coaches ran into London, at £12 per annum each, it became a very large sum for the Londoners to pocket, accounting for some thousands a year. Each coach was charged 12s 6d a week for washing and greasing the wheels; for every parcel or passenger had to be paid 2d for booking; the coachmen paid their takings into the London end, and thus the London proprietors had thousands always at their bankers.'[13]

Fowler might have added that sometimes town proprietors, having negotiated a rate for coach hire, would charge their partners a fraction above it. In all sorts of ways their opulence and influence allowed them to call the tune. For example, Brotherton, from Liverpool, was said to have 'got most . . . large inns under his control, and he would lay down his own practice: "I will build my own coaches, and will have such a price for them," he would say, "if you want to work . . . with me, I have no objection, but I shall find the coach" . . .'.[14]

Not that country proprietors were poor. Fowler described himself as 'a fair representative of middle-class life'. They had several irons in the fire. Most were in posting, many had farms (partly geared to maintaining their horses and inns). There was the inn trade and inn itself — often worth a great deal of money, and it had usually appreciated greatly in value. But few country proprietors acquired their wealth through coaches. Many innkeepers lost heavily on them. As early as 1827 Chaplin commented, 'I have not a shadow of a doubt that, were the coaching account of the nation kept regularly, the whole is decidedly a loss and the public have the turn'. Irish mail coaches were far more expensive to run than those on the mainland, because Irish innkeepers 'could not be induced to embark upon the trade'. In short, British innkeepers (and other country proprietors) were subsidising both public and Post Office.[15] Then why on earth did they do it? So long as there was a spin-off in meals one can understand why they might have

'A fair representative of middle-class life' — John K. Fowler,
innkeeper, White Hart, Aylesbury

accepted losses, but if this was no longer true for many of them why did these hard-headed businessmen continue to throw away their money? Many were only maintaining transport activities with their farm profits by the 1830s. But new coaches continued to be put on, mostly at a loss, and people kept them on even when they knew (and they did know) that matters could only worsen as railways expanded. It is all seemingly inexplicable.

William Wimberley, who as a settling agent knew the financial situation of coaching all too well, commented on the peculiar situation where 'persons will have coaches going whether they gain or lose; there is ... that strange system in the coaching interest, that persons will put on coaches merely for the sake of putting them on' and would keep them running unprofitably rather than allow others to take over their route. Christopher Kemplay had also noticed: 'very frequently an opposition has been carried on by the old coach masters from a sort of attachment to the road, a desire to keep it to themselves, and a spirit of party against all intruders and they have sometimes lost large sums of money'. William Horne, in explaining why proprietors persisted with unprofitable mails, claimed, 'the mail coach marks the house'. It was a status symbol — and so was the stage coach.[16]

One is drawn to the conclusion that this unique system was largely created and maintained by vanity and egotism. It was the Concorde of the age, a marvel, technically and aesthetically, but hopelessly uneconomic except to a few hard-headed 'town' proprietors.

In fact surprisingly little is known of the great London coachmasters. William Waterhouse was over thirty-five years in the business, owned 400 horses and the Swan with two Necks in 1827. Robert Gray operated from the Belle Sauvage, then the Bolt in Tun, Fleet Street; Robert Fagg was based at the Bell and Crown, Holborn, and Joseph Hearn, one of the few carriers in coaching, worked from the King's Arms, Snow Hill. Peter Mountain of the Saracen's Head, Snow Hill, followed his father and grandfather, who had started off in hackney coaches, eventually owning a large number. There were still a few in operation when Mountain took over for his mother, Sarah, in 1818. He had 200 horses by 1827. Mrs Ann Nelson took over management of the Bull, Aldgate, and the coaching business when her husband died, assisted by her son, John. Another son, Robert, had the Belle Sauvage, Ludgate Hill, entirely to himself and owned 400 horses in 1835.

Benjamin Worthy Horne, at twenty-four, took over the Golden Cross and some 800 horses from his father, William, who died at forty-five in 1828. He expanded the concern substantially and came to own or lease important London inns, including the Old Bell and the Cross Keys, Cheapside, and the George and Blue Boar, Holborn.

Edward Sherman was a self-made man. He came to London at the age of seventeen in 1793, too poor to pay for his ride from Berkshire, and obtained work at 12s a week. He grew wealthy mainly, apparently, by judicious dealings on the stock exchange, and a succession of marriages to three rich wives did nothing to hinder his progress. He bought the Bull and Mouth hotel, and rebuilt it at a cost of about £60,000. He became second largest coach proprietor in England, keeping about seventeen hundred horses at work and carrying on a business with annual returns estimated at more than half a million pounds.[17]

William Chaplin, the 'veritable Napoleon of coach proprietors', was born at Rochester, Kent, in 1787, son of a coachman-proprietor, and he himself started off driving the Dover *Union*. Marriage to the sister-in-law of James Edwards, 'one of the largest proprietors on the Kentish routes', proved useful. He and Edwards allied in many ventures in Kent. He came to horse more and more coaches, until by 1827 he owned between three to four hundred animals and the Spread Eagle, Gracechurch Street. By 1835 he owned 1,200 horses and the Swan with two Necks. In 1838 he horsed sixty-eight coaches with 1,800 horses, employing 2,000 men. He also acquired the Cross Keys, the White Horse, Fetter Lane, and opened the Spread Eagle coach office in Regent Circus.

Of provincial coachmasters like Brotherton even less is known. There were two Brothertons, old Bartholomew of Liverpool, who set up his nephew, Bartholomew, at the Castle Inn, Birmingham, in partnership with Tom Waddell, who between them came to have 'almost the whole coaching and parcels trade of the town'. Tom's father, William Waddell, son of a London oil merchant, had originally had a business connection with Piper of the Castle Inn, Birmingham, and then came to manage his posting business. When Piper died in 1802 Waddell had taken over the Castle and two years later moved to the Hen and Chickens until his death in 1836.

'During his occupancy,' Eliezer Edwards wrote, 'the posting and coaching attached to the place grew to a business of enormous magnitude and his name . . . became a household word . . . . As early as 1819 something like thirty coaches per day left the Hen and Chickens yard, and in the following fifteen years the number must have doubled.' In 1830 Waddell bought the Swan Hotel, working from there in conjunction with his son Thomas before mentioned.[18]

Bianconi was born in 1786 near Milan, son of the owner of a small silk mill. At fifteen Carlo was bound to a travelling vendor of cheap prints and accompanied him to Dublin, whence he was sent out selling them. He came to envy travellers who could afford to drive, and came to appreciate the need for better public communications.

In 1806 he set up in business as a carver and gilder and amassed capital through judicious bullion dealings during the Napoleonic wars which he used to begin his transport revolution in 1815. Horses were cheap after the war, and he bought up cheap jaunting cars thrown on the market because of a wartime carriage tax. He became a wealthy man, dominating Irish coaching from 1815 to 1865.

More is known of Bianconi, the 'wily Italian', than any other coach proprietor, even down to his favourite dishes — cockles, pig's head, and tripe — and his favourite phrases — 'By gor!' and other Irishisms pronounced with Italian accent. Respected and admired by public and employees alike, the 'Governor' was a good man to work for. In case of accident, sickness or old age incapacitating his men they were guaranteed full wages for life and their widows a pension. Orphans were educated and found work in his organisation. As an employer the Italian was strict but kindly and just. In fact he was something of a patriarchal despot — one employee dubbed him the 'Rajah of Longfield' — but he tolerated considerable liberty of speech from employees. He had a shrewd knowledge of character and was particularly astute at picking the right man for a job. A brilliant organiser, he was for ever on the go. He paid the closest attention to details, spending hours going over waybills.

As a man he had considerable humanity. During the famine years he gave employment, on his Longfield estate near Cashel, to all who applied, and was 'otherwise usefully beneficient'. He 'gave away a great deal of money in alms during his lifetime'. Highly thought of by his workforce and by the Irish, especially the humbler classes, who derived great benefit from

Charles Bianconi

his cars, he was able to boast that not the slightest injury had ever been done to his property, and never, in that troubled land, had any of his cars ever been stopped, even when conveying mails through disturbed districts.[19]

Dynamism, sagacity and an ability to manage men, including partners, were the most common characteristics of successful coach proprietors, along with a keen knowledge of horseflesh. Many provincial proprietors had the stamp of Richard 'Dickie' Wood in Doncaster, who had over 200 horses. He was 'one of the best known and most popular men in Doncaster. He was a rather stout, fresh-looking, good-natured fellow, wearing a top hat and a high white choker, and was never as happy as when ... entertaining his friends.'[20] William Waddell was 'a man of great energy and shrewdness', Benjamin Horne had 'exceptional energy and vitality', Mrs Nelson was 'cheerful, active and bustling'; Chaplin was possessed of 'immense energy, an equable temperament and great sagacity', with 'a very good knowledge of the animals he governed as well as the bipeds with whom he was associated'. But they all possessed a ruthless streak, including Bianconi. Sherman was said to have been a 'hard, even a mean man'. Horne was 'ruthless in the matter of business'. The empires of Chaplin, Sherman and Horne grew so rapidly that it seems unlikely they simply met growing demand but muscled in on territory of existing proprietors. Horne, apparently, was always good enough to make rivals a proposal to share the traffic of any road he intended to 'cut in' on, but, failing acceptance, the smaller man usually found himself beaten by the 'tenacity and longer purse of his rival'. Once he went down overnight and bought up all the horses at one stage. Next day the rival coach was brought to an ignominious halt.[21] It was a case of accept or be ruined. And there seems little doubt that London and provincial coachmasters cynically manipulated country proprietors operating the unremunerative 'middle ground'.

A detailed study of these men would make interesting reading, but the lives of the great British proprietors, their characters and personalities, are less well documented than Bianconi's. We get occasional opinions. 'A better man never breathed' than Richard Costar, Bayzand reckoned. The younger Bartholomew Brotherton was said to be a 'gentleman in every sense of the word — kind, affable and generous'. Matthew Outhwaite, an enterprising Leeds proprietor with about 200 horses, as well as being 'a short, stout, fresh comfortable-looking man' was 'a good and kind master'.[22] Chaplin was said to be well liked by his employees, although Thomas Cross did not hold him in such high regard. Chaplin, he explained, had a 'soft oily expression that procured him the soubriquet "Bite 'em sly". He possessed also a sort of playful sarcasm ... under which he disguised his real object ...'

(According to Ben Holmes, his nickname was actually 'Billy-bite-em-slow', from a portrait of Chaplin leading a favourite horse of that name. Both are equally unflattering.)

Nor could George Denman, toll collector at Kensington Gate, be expected to have been among Chaplin's admirers. In an altercation over a wrong toll ticket Denman took hold of Chaplin's carriage horses, whereupon the coach magnate horsewhipped him 'severely'. True, turnpike keepers were often 'sour, uncivil fellows who seemed to delight in making themselves obnoxious to travellers'. Dickens has the elder Weller saying, 'They're all on 'em men as has met with some disappointment in life, consequence of vich they retires from the world, and shuts themselves up in pikes, partly with the view of being solitary, and partly to revenge themselves on mankind by takin' tolls.'[23] But there are limits. Chaplin was fined 12*s* and costs. It was hardly the action of a man of 'equable temperament', rather of one who exhibited a certain shortness of temper when thwarted. Perhaps he was rarely thwarted.

'Competition from steam vessels'. *British Library*

As to the humanity of British proprietors, there was nothing on the scale of Bianconi's sickness benefits, care of orphans or pensions, other than those paid out to Post Office guards. An ageing coachman might be kept on as spare coachman or guard; the funeral expenses of a man killed at work might be paid, but that was about it. So far as is possible to ascertain, most coaching personnel, apart from Post Office guards, were left to shift for themselves when railways shattered their existence. British proprietors also expressed less concern for the travelling public than Bianconi, and virtually none for poorer travellers.

Perhaps we are being unfair to British proprietors in comparing them critically with Bianconi. Too little is known about them. It is uncertain, for example, how much of their wealth stemmed from coaching and how much from other sources such as inns. Perhaps profits from coaching were as slight for them as for country proprietors and there was little for philanthropy. And certainly British coaching was more costly than Irish in terms of horses and feed, vehicles and labour. Above all, Bianconi had one great advantage over his British counterparts. Although road tolls were an equal burden, there were no taxes on Irish transport.

These taxes became increasingly unfair as competition increased. Particularly inequitable was competition from steam vessels, which, in the 1830s, began to affect trade seriously. They paid no mileage duty at all, so the fare of the best cabin was half the duty alone for the same distance by coach. Even more unfair, if a coach was licensed for a certain number of passengers, mileage duty must be paid on that number whether the coach was full or not. Railways, significant competitors from about 1836, paid duty only on passengers actually carried and then at a lower rate.[24]

The accidents (relatively rare in Ireland) which the public railed against were equally galling to proprietors. They created a bad image and involved them in considerable expense through destroyed stock, vehicles and lawsuits. Proprietors of the Leeds–Huddesfield mail had to pay out £400 damages on one day. It was sometimes rather hard on proprietors, defending counsel pleaded. '. . . of all persons in the world, coach proprietors were the most hardly dealt with; for they were subjected to lawsuits, damages, and costs for what ... they could not prevent. All that they could do was to appoint a steady driver, and provide good horses — this the defendants had done.'[25]

There *were* proprietors careless about who they employed, the horses they used, and the condition of their vehicles, but many were not, and accidents came as an extra burden to them. Accounts of diligence in attending to needs of the injured, including paying medical expenses, are frequent enough.

13

HORSES NOR WHIPS SPARED

Whatever the faults and failings of the system, the British prided themselves that theirs was the best. Inevitably the French bore the greatest burden of contempt and superiority. 'The whole equipment is so unsightly,' one observer wrote of the *diligence* (and of the German *Eilwagen*), equivalent of the stage coach, '— the rope harness so rude — the horses without blinkers, look so wild — there is so much bluster and noise in the postillion ...; in England one would have travelled at nearly twice the rate with one-tenth of the noise'.[1] 'Bluster and noise' were anathema. Frenchmen could not even get their mail coach (*malle-poste*) along quietly. Although 'exceedingly adroit in the administration of plenty of noise and bustle in changing horses and getting along the road' with neither 'horses nor ... whips spared', the end result proved exertion misapplied. (In America, too, Dickens reckoned, 'the main thing to be done in all kinds of hostelering here, is to make as much noise as possible'.) 'There is plenty of galloping and rolling about, plenty of whipping and scolding,' a *Times* correspondent in France observed, 'but we miss the care and attention to the horses, the quiet and unobstrusive labour by which the power and energies of the team are reserved for that part of the road where they can be useful, and the cool determination to be in the "right place" at the "right time".' There was no comparison between the French 'trotting waggon' — although 'good enough in its way' — and the English mail coach.[2]

There were no outsides on European vehicles (a tradition which possibly accounts for the paucity of double-deck buses

'Galloping and rolling about' — the French *malle-poste*. *British Library Newspaper Library*

there) because long journeys — five days by diligence from Paris to Marseilles — would have been unbearable under the rigours of the Continental climate. It *was* more practicable (just) in milder British climes on relatively shorter journeys. It was not merely a question of cost, according to one French visitor. 'The desire to breathe ... fresh air, rather than economical considerations, induces even the richest English to give preference to outside places.' Europeans thought it all rather odd.

Since Continental practice meant 'inside only', the British abroad precipitated themselves into the *coupé*, immediately behind the horses, the section with most fresh air and the best view. It held only three people, another boon for Anglo-Saxons ever fearful of mixing with Latins. It was also the most expensive. The diligence was further divided into the *berline*, holding eight, the *rotonde*, holding six, and the cramped *banquette* above the *coupé*, with space for three or four.

Travellers who frequently expressed horror at sharing with three others in British coaches were overwhelmed when squashed in with six or eight foreigners. 'The French milliner who occupies one of the corners, begins to remove the greasy pieces of paper which have enveloped her locks ...,' records an Englishman as a diligence approaches Paris. 'She removes the "Madras" of dubious hue which has bound her head for the last five-and-twenty hours, and replaces it by the black velvet bonnet, which bobbing against your nose has hung from the diligence roof since your departure from Boulogne. The old lady ..., who has been sucking bonbons and smells dreadfully of annisette ... looks wistfully at the company for an instant, and then places her handkerchief before her mouth; her eyes roll strangely about for an instant, and you hear a faint clattering noise: the old lady has been getting ready for teeth, which had lain in her basket among the bonbons, pins, oranges, pomatum, bits of cake, lozenges, prayer books, peppermint water, copper money, and false hair .... The sallow-faced English lord, who has been drunk ever since we left Boulogne yesterday ... swears that he rejoices to leave the cursed diligence, and is sick of the infernal journey.'[3]

There was little of the aesthetic. When Nimrod first saw the Paris–Lille diligence approaching it was 'something ... like a haystack on wheels ... how slow it moves'. In fact the average speed was about 5 m.p.h. 'Much stopping, much drinking, much swearing, and very little progress,' was the Duke of Beaufort's recollection of travelling by diligence. Nimrod remarked on the 'good quarter of an hour spent in changing horses and in jaw'.

Horses were more specialised in France, certain breeds generally doing certain jobs. Diligences were invariably pulled by 'heavy snorting Norman stallions' ('one remove from the cart horse'). The French were incapable of putting horses together. One aghast enthusiast saw an 'off-wheeler about the height of a camel, ... near-wheeler about the size of a Welsh pony, and the "unicorn" a miserable animal of the Galloway size'.[4]

If British ostlers were 'low fellows' they seem to have been a cut above the French. 'The swearing of ostlers is never heard at the relays' in England, one Frenchman admitted. Nor was there that 'hallooing of conductors which in France falls so disagreeably on the ears of travellers'. The French *cocher* was

'A haystack on wheels': a French *diligence*, 1835. *British Library*

no coachman but a mere driver and a 'peasant' to boot. 'There is a person *thrashing* on the top of your haystack!' Nimrod remarked sarcastically. 'But it is only the fellow who drives; his pig whip is never quiet for a moment. Hark! How heavy it falls! He hits first one horse, then another, and what is the consequence? Why . . . with no command over their mouths, having only one pair of reins to five horses . . ., no sooner does he hit his nearside horse than the coach follows that horse to the offside of the road and vice versa.'

There was little intercourse between drivers and passengers on European conveyances. Thus they tended to remain in the peasant class from which they came and were rather 'rude' fellows, not least in their language. To 'swear like a *cocher*' is still a French idiom. D'Haussez found it perplexing that in England the 'place most in request — one knows not wherefore — is to the left of the coachman; it is considered as the place of honour, and is reserved for the fashionable, and even for Lords, who do not disdain to travel thus'.

There were two ways of driving the diligences (and the *malle poste*) — by *cocher* from the box, or by *postillion* — equally 'leather-lunged' — sitting on one of the horses. He also drove 'after the manner of an English waggoner' — by voice and whip, which fell 'with great severity on his leaders'. Postil-

lions' boots made the British laugh. They were massive reinforced structures to protect feet and legs if the horse fell. Some
tied the boots to the saddles and climbed into them; others
came clumping out hardly able to walk. Nimrod was particularly amused to see 'an Herculean-looking fellow — a
regular Jack the Giant Killer — in seven-league boots, strad-
dling along like a second Colossus of Rhodes, with his pig-whip
in the air, shouting at the top of his voice . . .' stumbling after
his escaping horses. The postillion was 'a perfect nondescript
— half sailor, half soldier — a touch of the waggoner and a good
deal of the labourer . . .'

There was no comparison with Britain. 'A portly, good-
looking coachman seated on a very high coach-box, well
dressed, wearing white gloves, a nosegay in his buttonhole,
and his chin enveloped in an enormous cravat, drives four
horses perfectly matched and harnessed, and as carefully
groomed.'

Dickens, for all his criticism, found British coachmen a
great improvement on American. In his journey from Cinc-
cinnati he found 'The frequent change of coachmen works no
change or variety . . . . He is always dirty, sullen and taciturn.
If he be capable of smartness of any kind, moral or physical, he
has a faculty of concealing it which is truly marvellous. He
never speaks to you . . . and if you speak to him, he answers (if
at all) in monosyllables. He points out nothing on the road,
and seldom looks at anything: being, to all appearance,
thoroughly weary of it and of existence generally . . . . He
always chews, and always spits, and never encumbers himself
with a pocket-handkerchief. The consequences to the box
passenger, especially when the wind blows towards him are
not agreeable.'

The only coachman he met with any sparkle drove him on a
hair-raising but hilarious journey to Fredericksburgh. 'He is a
negro — very black indeed. He is dressed in a course pepper-
and-salt suit excessively patched and darned . . . grey
stockings, enormous unblacked high-low shoes, and very short
trousers. He has two odd gloves . . . . He has a very short whip,
broken in the middle and bandaged up with string. And yet he
wears a low-crowned, broad-brimmed, hat: faintly shadowing
forth a kind of insane imitation of an English coachman.'

'They were massive reinforced structures': a French postillion, and
boots. *British Library*

The journey led over bridges of loose planks 'which tilt up as
the wheels roll over them' and through the river 'full of holes,
so that half a horse is constantly disappearing unexpectedly,
and can't be found again for some time'. The road itself was 'a
series of alternate swamps and gravel-pits'. On one steep bank
the black driver became 'louder, more vigorous, and more
loquacious between each desperate attempt by the horses.

' ''Pill!

' ''Pe-e-e-ill!

' ''Hi, Jiddy, Jiddy, Pill!

' ''Ally Loo! Hi, Jiddy, Jiddy, Pill. Ally Loo!''

'Finally, with eyes starting out of his head, he found the
successful formula.

' ''Lee, den, Lee, dere. Hi, Jiddy, Jiddy, Pill, Ally Loo. Lee-e-
e-e-e!''

'They run up the bank, and go down again on the other side
at a fearful pace. It is impossible to stop them, and at the
bottom there is a deep hollow full of water. The coach rolls

frightfully. The insides scream. The mud and water fly about us. The black driver dances like a madman. Suddenly we are all right by some extraordinary means and stop to breathe . . . .

'One last hole — ''Easy. Easy den. Ease steady. Hi Jiddy. Pill. Ally. Loo'' but never ''Lee'' ' and they were through, taking two and a half hours for the ten-mile journey, 'breaking no bones, though bruising a great many'.

Of course, coaching was a more rugged business outside Britain, especially outside Europe — bad roads, extremes of climate . . . a different clientele. As late as 1875 a colonial visitor entertained English enthusiasts aboard the fashionable London–Guildford summer coach with stories of travels in the 'Australian bush, where coaching exists as a necessity, and is of the most primitive kind'. He told one story of 'a rough traveller . . . from Bendigo Diggings, . . . uproariously drunk . . ., brandishing his loaded revolver about in a most uncomfortable manner. No one dared take it from him without a flare-up, so they adopted a safer course by getting him to sit on the edge of the roof, and the coachman purposely driving into a deep rut shot the drunken brawler off on to his head . . . . This was in the night-time, and, of course, no one stopped to pick him up.'[5]

Whatever criticisms were made of some inns, foreigners were highly impressed. They were one of the 'wonders of English civilisation'. 'In many . . . larger towns they are magnificent, and . . . good and well supplied in the smallest,' d'Haussez remarked. 'In the greater part . . . servants are in livery, and in all, their attendance is prompt and respectable', in contrast to Nimrod's experience in Gravelines, where the waiting-maid was in 'wretched dishabille and wooden shoes'.

'On their arrival, travellers are received by the master of the house, whose decent dress indicates a respectful feeling towards strangers.' It was this attention which Englishmen looked back on nostalgically when railways brought those 'caravanserai's' sporting the 'Frenchified word *Hotel*' and the old inns disappeared. In them 'the guests know nothing of the managers,' Fowler protested, 'nor do the managers know anything of their guests. . . . No welcome attends you . . ., no expression of regret at your departure awaits you. . . . Nothing, in fact, to associate the traveller with his Inn, or any pleasing

'A much more rugged business outside Britain'. *Julia Holmes*

recollection of the agreeable evening with town or country gossip, over the cigar in the comfortable bar parlour with "mine host".'[6]

Nowhere else was there to be found this same personal attention. On arriving at an American inn, for example, 'you excite no kind of sensation whatever, come how you will', and, worse, the servant 'always assumes with you the manners of an equal'.[7]

However, as we have seen, the benefits of English inns did not come cheap. 'Your discontent does not commence till the exorbitant bill proves that such attentions, far from being disinterested, are ... dearly charged for,' wrote d'Haussez. 'Seldom do you separate from your host with a reciprocation of politeness.' But British innkeepers were a thick-skinned lot, for 'notwithstanding the coldness with which his attentions are received, the landlord does not cease to remain by ... the traveller till his carriage is in motion'. Clearly British inns catered for an exclusive wealthy few, and it was these men who looked back so nostalgically. Travellers of more limited means were understandably less enamoured. Although foreign inns lacked British style they were perhaps more in tune with the needs (and purses) of travellers, as possibly was coaching generally. One of Nimrod's criticisms of the Calais–Boulogne conveyance was its cheapness! — 'the fares are too low to do it well. What can five francs, or four shillings and twopence, in and out, do for twenty-four miles of very severe road?'

Equally, although foreign drivers lacked the panache of British coachmen, the Frenchman was Nimrod admitted, invariably 'a civil fellow to his passengers without expecting to be paid for it'. One wonders, too, about excessive criticism of the French system. It was (and is) a long-established tradition to mock 'Johnny Frenchman'. Its proximity, obviously brought it under closest scrutiny ... but could it also have been because the French came nearest to challenging British 'superiority'? D'Haussez had the effrontery to claim that although roads, horses and harness *were* better in England 'nonetheless our carriages take no more time in performing a given distance', and the 'malle-poste from Paris to Bordeaux takes no longer to perform the journey than the English mail ... from London to Edinburgh — the same distance'.

Apperley was quick to condemn the 'absurd comparison drawn between English and French travelling by Baron d'Haussez', but it is noticeable that he counters the Frenchman's claims with scathing anecdotes about diligences, whereas on the relative merits of *malle-poste* and mail he is significantly silent. In 1862 General Morin claimed 'the *malle-poste* between Paris and Brussels was timed to be accomplished at ... from fifteen to sixteen kilometres per hour' [9·4–10 m.p.h.] and the English mails, of which the English 'had long boasted the speed, were at that time far surpassed by ours, and travelled at the utmost from twelve to fourteen kilometres per hour [7·5–8·75 m.p.h.] in spite of the brilliant appearance of their four horses and the unvarying dignity of the coachman'.

Much poring over 'old books of the London General Post Office' followed to show that the 'public mail service in England was not surpassed by the French and that what is set down as a ''boast'' ... was only a statement of fact' and, further, 'many of the stage coaches surpassed the mail coaches in speed'.[8]

This was probably a chauvinistic interpretation. Significantly the Duke of Beaufort, himself a keen amateur during the coaching era, later admitted *malle postes* 'fully equalled the pace at which ours travelled', including stoppages, and were 'quite up to the Devonport Quicksilver Mail, the Exeter Telegraph, or the Shrewsbury Wonder, viz. eleven miles an hour'. Since these English coaches never actually achieved 11 m.p.h. (but 10·2, 9·7 and 10·3 m.p.h., including stops) the implication is that the French were faster.

That is not to say that French *horses* were faster (although they may have been, since they only did five-mile stages). But, apart from stopping more to change horses, the French otherwise stopped less. *Malle postes* 'were inconveniently fast to the traveller', the Duke wrote, 'for as their changes of horses were effected in forty-five seconds, he had not time to get out to stretch his legs, excepting at long intervals when at a post office bags had to be taken in or out'. The very best time quoted for changing horses in England, with many men on hand, was a minute and a half. For all they were 'inconveniently fast', the Duke did conclude: 'From Calais through . . . to Marseilles by *malle-poste* was something like travelling, as good as going from London to Edinburgh or Glasgow by the mail, and in a much more comfortable carriage.' Significantly the British Post Office was, in 1832, seriously considering adopting the French *malle-post* system.

If Apperley exaggerated the diligences' defects, clearly they *were* slower and less stylish than British stage coaches. But they had other advantages. A *Times* correspondent, in writing of the accident to Eliza Semirot, rather patronisingly commented, 'the public conveyances of her own country may be less handsome and less rapid than ours' but, he had to admit, 'they are probably much safer'.

Five important causes of accidents in Britain were broken axles and poles, wheels coming off, runaway horses, and the coach overrunning horses on hills. Without the skid pan the wheelers could only hold back by a chain from their collars to the pole. This put an impossible burden on their necks if the coach began to overrun, and their only course was to try to outrun it, often with disastrous results.

On every diligence a *méchanique*, wound up by the guard,

braked both rear wheels on every hill. Apperley admitted that
if adopted in Britain it would save more than 'three parts of the
accidents that occur to our fast coaches', but it rarely was. It
would also have held back runaway horses. It was rejected,
ostensibly and erroneously, on grounds of weight and cost and
that it would make horses lazy, but basically British coachmen
saw it as a cissy device. Similarly with breeching, which would
have helped wheelers hold back. Breeching rarely featured in
coach harness, partly because of cost but mostly because it did
not look 'natty'.

Poles rarely broke in France, because they were encased in
iron, wheels rarely came off because they had especially safe
linchpins, and axles were better designed so the coach would
continue upright after a breakage. These features could have
been redesigned on British coaches but rarely were. The law
was more severe in France too. In England the judiciary ful-
minated but rarely backed words with strong action. Apperley
drew attention to a widely distributed French poster declaring,
'Whereas the proprietor of the — Diligence did, by his neglect
. . . cause the death of two individuals: it is hereby ordered . . .
[he] shall not in future be allowed to have any diligences
running . . . in this Department. Moreover criminal and civil
action shall be brought against him, to punish him for his base
neglect and to indemnify the sufferers by a pecuniary com
pensation.'

The French system had other good points. Drivers and
postillions rarely drove or rode more than an hour at one time
(although the *conducteur* of the diligence went through,
sleeping as best he could). They were granted pensions after
twenty-five years' service. Horses, too, underbred though they
may have been, lasted much longer.

It would be foolish to attempt rigid comparisons from a few
anecdotal accounts, and what is particularly needed are
comparisons of cost. But perhaps the French system served
French economy and people better than the British system the
British. The fashionable interest the upper crust took in
coaching forced style and pace upon it, making the whole
system ruinously expensive (and dangerous) and more exclusive than need have been. More slower, cheaper, safer, long-
distance coaches might have served Britain's interests better,

and just might have helped alleviate intense working-class poverty in the rural south by enabling more people to move to industrial growth areas. Bianconi's system was more in tune with the needs of the native economy and people. His cars were aimed at carrying poor people — there was the 'lordly mail coach for the "quality"' — and he made a fortune from sticking to this principle, even when the 'quality' became attracted to his cars. The Italian wrought a social revolution, 'contributing as much to the progress and prosperity of Ireland as any public man' of the nineteenth century, and perhaps not least by enabling the poor to leave that blighted isle. The British system was very much geared to the 'quality', but where slower, cheaper coaches *were* put on and proprietors resisted temptations to be 'flash' they were successful. The 'New Company' coaches on the Bristol road operated such vehicles, carrying six inside. Miss Fromont, who kept the King's Head, Thatcham, near Newbury, was the principal proprietor. She 'managed her coaching business with considerable ability, and from the slow rate at which they travelled, her horses lasted much longer, and the wear and tear was very much diminished as compared with the stock of her opponents; indeed it was considered that the New Company paid as well as any on the road', and this despite the rule: 'no fees' to the coachman.[9]

14

RASH TOM, LITTLE BALL AND SPICEY JACK

Men who work in transport, particularly those on the move, seem to have a high level of job satisfaction. They grumble and complain like the rest of us, but as a body they appear to like their work more than most. So it was with coachmen, for 'although the work was extremely hard — exposure to every change of weather, the unflagging strain upon the attention, the grave responsibility incurred by the charge of so many lives — there was something so fascinating in the work, . . . there were few instances of their relinquishing the ribbons except from physical incapacity'.[1] There was the variety of seeing new places and people; changing scenes and seasons, as well as incidents on the road.

In coaching days there were incidents a-plenty. Some were trivial. The York mail guard had a surprise when he began unloading at the Cross Keys, Hull, at six o'clock on a cold December morning in 1822. He discovered a hen roosting on top which had apparently travelled all the way from York, undisturbed by the motion.[2] Another guard had a different surprise. Mailbags were often dropped and picked up without stopping at small sub-post offices. At night it was not unusual for a sub-postmaster to drop them on the passing coach from his bedroom. Once, at an office in Caithness, on a dark rainy night, the guard was handed what he supposed were mailbags, but a little later the astonished postmaster was again roused by the tootle of the horn and an angry shout. 'Hey, mon! Gie's the bags an' tak in yer breeks!'[3]

Less trivial was the well known story of the escaped lioness which leapt from the darkness to tear at a leader of the *Quick-*

silver. This was a rare occurrence, but horses were sometimes troubled by dogs. On one occasion a fierce mastiff seized the thigh of a leader of the Durham — Newcastle *True Briton* and 'so firmly did the savage animal keep his hold . . . it was found necessary to nearly choke him . . . ere he would quit his merciless grasp. The horse was so dreadfully lacerated as to be quite unable to proceed.' A like incident occurred when three bulldogs suddenly leapt upon the Portsmouth mail leaders by the Devil's Punchbowl, near Hindhead. The horses, in their desperate struggles, broke the harness and went over the edge, taking the ferocious dogs with them, but not, fortunately, the coach.[4]

Passengers provided most of the distractions and amusements. Foreigners were always entertaining, especially Frenchmen, with Waterloo not long past. One particularly tall monsieur travelled contentedly to Rochester. He alighted to stretch his legs until he read 'Cheapside' on the coach, when he flew into a violent rage.

'Vat,' he said, 'you put me here for? I pay de best price, and I will not be disgraced by riding *cheapside* of de coach.'

He refused to listen to the chuckled explanations, and finally, the joke wearing thin, the coach behind time and the passengers beginning to curse, he had to squash his long legs elsewhere, uncomfortable but happy that honour was satisfied.[5]

If some passengers, as seen by the crews, were odd or unpleasant, many were interesting and knowledgeable and not averse to chatting with them, which added to their education and gave them that cultured veneer and fund of anecdotes appreciated by others. It was not everyone in their milieu who could open a conversation: 'As the Duke, Admiral, Member, etc., was telling me yesterday . . .'. Jack Goodwin recalled, 'In my career for thirty-five years as a stage coach guard, I have carried passengers from the duke to the executioner.' It was the latter who most impressed him. 'I think about '31, when on the Lynn *Red Rover* to London, I had the patronage of Calcraft, who the previous day had executed an execution at Ely, on a poor unfortunate, for incendiarism. . . . He took his seat behind, alongside me . . . and I offered him a cigar, and addressed him by name. He replied I was mistaken. I told him I could not be mistaken, as I have seen him ''perform'' on three unfortunates at the Old Bailey a few weeks previous. Suffice, we fraternised, and then he opened his budget of executions.'[6]

The odd passenger falling off provided an occasional distraction. Particularly dramatic was the incident where Mr Walford, returning to London after a week's shooting in Oxford, in mounting the coach let off his gun and killed himself on the spot.[7] Passengers sometimes died *en route* of natural causes. The saddest story concerned Caroline Elms, a sickly fourteen-year-old, sent by her poor widowed mother to Exeter for the country air in May 1835. There she stayed with friends until on 8 January she wrote that her health was deteriorating and she wanted to die at home in London. Mrs Elms went for her.

The doctor in Exeter was adamant she should not be moved, but young Caroline was so insistent that they did set out. The girl was obviously fading, and at two o'clock in the morning the mother tried to keep her daughter's spirits up. 'You will yet reach London, and there I will resign you to the Almighty.'

'Resign me now, my dear mother,' whispered the girl, 'for I am going.'

Within a few moments Mrs Elms felt the girl breathe her last. For six hours she held Caroline, without telling the other passengers for fear the body would be taken and she left on the road without money or friends. The coach arrived at the Bell and Crown, Holborn, and Mrs Elms, much distressed, took her dead daughter home in a hackney coach.[8]

A body of a different description travelled in the *Mazeppa*. It was empty from Ross. 'When we got within two miles of our changing place, we ran over something. . . . The coach gave a great lurch. I took my lamp and went back. . . . Why, it was a bacon pig, twelve or fourteen score, in a sack.'

'Fowler, you must come and help,' Bayzand shouted to the coachman. 'I cannot move it myself.'

Fowler fastened the reins round his seat, and left the four horses, with much 'wo, wo, wo'ing' as he walked cautiously back. He had to return several times to quiet the restive animals. So it went on — back to the bacon, back to the horses — until the hog was made an inside passenger. Later they salted, dried and divided the pig between them. 'We pronounced it ... the best and by far the cheapest we ever had.'

Mason, a coachman on the Plymouth–Falmouth road was another who lived off the 'fat of the land'. He never need buy a duck for dinner. As he drove along he could twist his whip round the neck of one of a flock and bring it on to the coach without the slightest difficulty, to the huge delight of the passengers, an art less appreciated by the duck and its owner.[9]

Inn workers had distractions too — not always pleasant. A respectable-looking young woman with long brown hair and dark complexion booked in to the Mackworth Arms, Swansea, from the *Cambrian* in October 1816 on her way to Ireland. The following morning she was found a corpse, by her side a bottle of laudanum and a note: 'I have long determined that the best thing I could do was to put an end to the existence of a being where birth was unfortunate, and whose life has only been a series of pain to those persons who have hurt their health in endeavouring to promote her welfare. Perhaps to hear of my death will give you pain, but you will soon have the blessing of forgetting that such a creature ever existed as —' The name had been torn off.[10]

Generally the animation at an inn was more cheerful, with the constant bustle of comings and goings of coaches and people, distinguished, pleasant, awkward and peculiar — like

'He never need buy a duck for dinner.' *British Library*

the Reverend Edward Franks, who, when at the Woolpack, Doncaster, was, according to the landlady, Mrs Nichols, 'a very noisy customer. He rang the bells and called for chambermaid, waiter, ostler and boots' for no reason. He never went to bed, shouting 'Tally-ho' and other hunting noises all the night. For breakfast he took a pint of champagne! It was the same wherever he went. He used to ring the bell at five in the morning to ask the time. The Reverend Franks was quite mad.[11]

Then there was the elderly man, George Davis, who added spice to the life of maids in London inns by getting into their beds — during the day! He met his match at the Old Bell, Holborn. The cook without hesitation stripped the bedclothes down, and bundled him off to a magistrate.[12]

David Johnson had the honour of crashing his coach into Wordsworth's pony-chaise. James Arnold, his guard on the Whitehaven Mail, used to enjoy telling the tale: '. . . as we were slapping along and just coming to a sharpish turn . . . what should we see but somethin tall and grand tooling along, a little pony shay as cool as murder. "Oh! Lor, her's a smash," says I, and afore the words were out o' mi mouth crash went the shay all to smitherens, right through a dry wall, and slap went the driver over into a plantation, arms out and greatcoats a-flying. We thought for sure it was all over with 'im, but presently he picked hissel up uncommon tall again, and, says he, "I'll have this matter thoroughly investigated . . . ."

' "Jem," said coachie to I, very down like . . . "who do you think that is?"

' "Who! Who!! Davey," says I. "Why, who but the powit Wadsworth?" '

Arnold always chuckled to himself when he saw grand visitors rolling up to see Wordsworth. 'I've said, sly like, to myself, "Ah, gentlemen, you be going to see the powit, but you never had 'n call upon you unexpected like, on a flying visit over a wall." '[13]

Sometimes coaches got involved in demonstrations of public disfavour because of the people they carried — Poor Law Commissioners arriving in Lancashire to implement the rigorous new Poor Law system in 1837; blacklegs arriving to take the jobs of striking locals. In 1837 a group of convicts were being sent by coach from Worcester for transportation, but a mob of 'the most desperate characters of the city' lay in wait . . . and hurled stones and abuse. But for the police escort 'the intention of the mob to rescue the convicts would have been effected'. Another mob of about five hundred 'ruffians' had assembled farther along the coach's route, but a swift detour 'disappointed them'.

It was commonplace to transport convicts chained to the coach but it was not always to the taste of other passengers that 'persons of respectable character should be exposed to the necessity of riding cheek-by-jowl with thieves and murderers', one angry *Times* correspondent complained on finding the coach loaded with convicts; but the practice continued until railways brought more discreet transportation.[14]

There is no doubt some coachmen, their heads perhaps turned by the adulation of amateur whips, chambermaids, farmers' daughters, thought themselves extremely fine fellows. There was 'above all . . . the admiration bestowed upon the "great" man . . . and his "appointments", his unexceptional "tops" [boots], the folds of the companion shawl, the magical twist of the long lash around the spiral handle as he threw it to the "helper" . . . which "trick" still continued to excite the applause of the bystanders. Then again with what inimitable importance would he lounge into the inn and condescend to "trifle" with the ever-ready and tempting lunch; with what a racy Falstaffian humour did he joke, and how would the smart and rosy hostess and her daughter . . . giggle and blush . . .'.[15]

However, there was no shortage of those who enjoyed taking them down a peg or two. One day a farm boy stopped the Birmingham day coach and asked Jim Howell in a very yokel-like manner, 'ef he'd a rome for tre insid passengers?'

'Yes, my dear boy, plenty of room,' replied Howell.

'Fur tre insid?'

'Yes, yes. Make haste.'

'Did you understand, sur?'

'Oh, yes, three inside passengers.'

'Tree.'

'Oh, yes, yes, do be quick, my good boy.'

'He be sure he ha got rume?'

'The "great" man' — a 'long' coachman. *British Library Newspaper Library*

'Why, how many more times am I to tell you?'

'Wal, ef I dos here o' anybody do want to go, I lit ye know.'

Joey Stephens was a show-off. One day he was airing his knowledge of driving to a young dandy. 'Now, do you think, if I set these horses at full gallop, . . . I could stop them before we got to that tree?'

'No,' said the young man.

Stephens set the team at full speed and stopped them at the tree. On board was a Quaker (Quakers featured frequently in coaching lore) who got off at Newbury. Stephens asked for his fee.

'No, friend,' he said, 'if thee hadst been a little stronger in thy head, and not so strong in the arms, I should have given thee a shilling. I shall now give it to thy guard.'[16]

Rarely did anyone got the better of Tim Healy, who drove Bianconi's Cork–Limerick car. Charles Cahill remembered how some playful Cork boys behind once surrepticiously extracted the breakfast of meat sandwiches from Tim's pocket and ate them. When breakfast time came Tim examined his pocket, but found no parcel. He looked at Cahill with a peculiar smile.

'What's the matter, Tim?'

'Begorra, sir,' he said loudly, 'last night . . . I told my wife, Molly, how two dirty blackguard dogs had run out of a house and tried to bite my horses' legs ∴. going down the hill of Fermoy. Now, Molly being a bit of a "ganus", sir, she said, "Tim, darlint, give me a shillin' till I go to the pothecarry's shop, and so, sir, she . . . bought a dose of arsenic and laid it over the bread and buther and the mate, and bade me throw that to the blackguard dogs the next time they dared to bite the legs of my horses; but upon my sowl, gintlemen, both the bread and mate are gone.' He turned to the young Cork wags with his peculiar smile. 'And I don't know who in the world has taken it.'

The lads were immediately taken ill and begged Tim to stop, which he did by a cabin where they were boiling potatoes. He advised them to drink the potato water, considered an excellent emetic in Ireland, which they did with great avidity.

The draught proved very effective and Tim addressed the woebegone youths with compassionate sarcasm: 'Now ye may get on the car agin, but please bring nurses with ye the next time ye come travelling, for sure, ye 're not fit to be out on the road alone.'

Coach crews were a close-knit group. They loved to talk about each others' eccentricities and adventures. They ribbed each other mercilessly. Ringrose drove the mail from Cambridge to Huntingdon and back. One summer morning at dawn a donkey lay down in the road, causing such a dust the leaders took fright and upset the mail. Poor Ringrose was chaffed about it so frequently, being asked whether he had met the donkey that morning, he was nearly driven off the road.

'These long coachmen loved a joke dearly,' Lord Algernon remembered, 'and never forgot to name it if you happened to touch anything when driving.'

Charles Ward used to recount the tale of how when he was driving the Devonport–London *Telegraph* in opposition to the *Tally-ho*, driven by William Harbridge, and he arrived first, 'My guard . . . hurried home, and as the other coach passed he called out and asked them to stop and have some supper; they

'The leaders took fright.'

also passed my home. ... I was sitting at the window, smoking, and offered them a cigar as they passed — a joke they did not, of course, much relish.'[17]

It was generally all very amicable, engendering a spirit of friendly rivalry, although some coachmen became deadly serious. Slugg remembered one day, as *North Star* and *Royal Bruce* changed at Garstang, the coachmen started fighting. On another occasion, as the *Red Rover* overhauled the *Endeavour* Birmingham–London the guard waggishly laid hold of a wheeler's ears as if to say, 'Come along.' The coachman was not amused and cut savagely at the guard with his whip.[18]

Coachmen and guards were often given nicknames because of quirks of character or appearance. 'Rash Tom' Holtby drove the Edinburgh mail from York. 'Little' Ball drove the crack Southampton *Telegraph* and later the Oxford–Southampton. 'Happy Jack' Goodwin we have met before. Another musical guard, Tom Botrill, of the *Eclipse Tally-ho*, was always 'Rory' Bottrill. Of the many fine key-bugle players he was said to be unrivalled. He played 'Rory o' More' so exquisitely that Rory became his name.[19] Richard Blight was 'Father' Blight on account of his thirty-two children. Several coachmen were prefixed 'Gentleman' because of their sartorial elegance, their politeness of manner or their origins, sometimes all three. 'Gentleman' Marsh drove the *Crown Prince*, and 'Gentleman' Wood, also on the London–Birmingham road, was 'a handsome roguish-looking man. He wears a white hat, his boots are brilliantly polished [They were in fact wellingtons] ... his drab greatcoat is faultlessly clean, and the dark blue handkerchief is daintily tied. His whiskers are carefully brushed forward and curled, the flower in the buttonhole is as fresh as if that instant plucked ...'.[20]

John Hennesy of the Stamford coach — 'not by any means a lively or amusing fellow' — was 'Saddler Jack'. Then there was 'Spicey Jack' Everett of the Warwick *Crown Prince*, who always dressed in a 'slap-up' fashion. Tim Healey was known as 'Lord Gort', although no one knew why. Perhaps it was because he was a 'paragon driver' — sober as a judge, a man assiduous in saying his prayers, polite and kind to all. Once, a donkey-cart driver, caught unawares by Tim's arrival, after making frantic efforts to pull over, finished up heading straight for the car. Tim, with great skill, avoided a collision, but, instead of the abuse which might have been expected, simply called out good-humouredly, 'Shure, you did it as well as you could.'

Then there was William Bowers, probably the only black coachman in Britain. He did not take all that kindly to his soubriquet and frequently explained that he was only called Black Will 'by blackguards; gentleman calls me Mr Bowers'.

At the other end of the scale there was 'Jerry the Royal', a porter at Clonmel. He was the official porter, but had many irregular competitors who skirmished around when a car arrived. Jerry had a palate defect so when he impressed upon clients he was the 'rale' porter it came out as *royal*.

Coaches were given nicknames too, often affectionate — the *Subscription* became the Old Scrippy — but sometimes highsounding names were replaced by something more akin to reality. The Liverpool–London *Royal Umpire* was more familiarly known as the 'Lazy Liverpool' and the Liverpool

Mercury the 'Lousy Liverpool'. The *Hirondelle* was the 'Iron Devil'.

Alas, British soubriquets lacked the delicious colonial rich-ness of Australians — 'Cabbage Tree' Ned Devine, 'Ointment' Taylor, 'Big Joe' Hirschberg, 'Silent Bob' Bates, 'Jim the Grumbler'. Nor, surely, could British coachmen have capped Mick Dougherty's yarn. He was telling a lady box passenger how he had trained a kangaroo to collect a mailbag thrown from the coach, open it and deliver its contents to surrounding homesteads. The woman was less than convinced, when, on turning a bend, an old male kangaroo was visible standing by the track. 'Nothing today, Jack,' called out Dougherty, cracking his whip, whereupon the kangaroo turned and bounded off into the bush.[21]

15

DYING BY INCHES

'Mr Bayzand,' said a passenger to the coachman of the *Oxonian*, 'if your head never aches till the railways come, it will be a long time.' By which he meant the new-fangled railroad would never catch on. The other passengers agreed, but old Bayzand knew he was doomed. 'Whether you want them or not, you'll be obliged to have them sooner or later, I can tell you.'

So it turned out. Every little railway failure raised coaching spirits, but soon it was undeniable that stagecoaches were finished. The opening of a new line on a coach route led almost immediately to its being taken off the road. Twenty-eight coaches had gone by 1832 as a result of the Liverpool & Manchester Railway, representing a revenue loss to coaching interests of £8,384 a year.[1] The story was repeated with increasing momentum throughout the 1830s. 'Till lately upwards of seventy coaches passed through Hounslow daily,' reported the *Times* of 4 April 1839, 'but now there are only nine or ten.'

Coaches hung on as fillers before a line was complete, but by 1840 the heart was ripped out of the network. By June 1844 the *Illustrated London News* was describing once proud mails as those 'reliques of departed days'.

The swift end of the coaching era had a dramatic effect upon coaching personnel. Edward Corbett summed up a truism, the poignancy of which we are again experiencing today. 'It is always a melancholy thing to see any class of men suddenly deprived of their means of subsistence from no fault of their own. It is very easy to say that if one trade fails another must be found, and to some political economists this appears to be a sufficient solution . . .; but it by no means has that effect upon the sufferers. A man who has thoroughly learned one handicraft can very seldom become as proficient in any other.'

For Post Office guards there was no problem. They simply transferred to the railways, carrying on much the same function at the same salary. Philip Salt explained to a select committee how he had been guard to the Liverpool, Chester, Manchester and Yarmouth mails before going on the railway in 1837, from Birmingham to Liverpool or Manchester and back each day. He travelled on top with the bags, taking up and leaving them off as before, going three days and resting the fourth.[2]

No one asked him whether he and his fellows enjoyed the change. Dickens thought not. On a railway journey back to London he remarked on the 'dejected and disconsolate demeanour of the Post Office guard'.

He dismounted 'slowly and sadly from his post, and looked mournfully about him as if in a dismal recollection of the old roadside public house — the blazing fire — the glass of foaming ale — the buxom handmaid and admiring hangers-on of tap room and stable all honoured by his notice; and retiring a little apart, stood leaning against a signal-post, surveying the engine with a look of continued affliction and disgust which no words can describe . . . it was plain to see . . . he felt his office and himself had alike no business there, and were nothing but an elaborate practical joke'.[3]

Some preferred to have nothing to do 'with the new-fangled monster, and quit the Post Office. James Arnold became landlord of the Ferry Hotel, Windermere, where he would sometimes take down his horn, give it an old-style coaching blast and relate again how they sent the 'powit Wadsworth' flying over the wall.

Some stagecoach guards went on to railways too, but many gave up their transport connections. William Bayzand became janitor at the Radcliffe Camera in Oxford. He never forgot those brief, happy years as *Mazeppa* guard and wrote his reminiscences in 1884 at the age of seventy-five.

The final trip proved too much for some, like Frisby, who drove the last *Lark* from Leicester to Nottingham on 23 May 1840, following the opening of the Midland Counties line. He had driven it for many years, a prudent, sober, careful coach-man respected for his civility. 'He was perfectly sober, but greatly excited at the circumstances of its being the last trip of his pet coach, and very imprudently took up a greater number of outside passengers than . . . warranted or licensed to carry.' From Loughborough he put the horses into a reckless gallop and the coach went over on a dangerous turn. Frisby was crippled for life, and among the dead was James Pearson, another coachman recently thrown out of work by the rail-way, on a nostalgic trip, Frisby handing him the ribbons for a spell.[4]

Others hung on to coaching as long as they could. The West Country, where railway development was slower, became a 'warm corner for coaching' for a few years. Top coachmen flocked there. Some stuck with the coaches into the recesses of Wales and Scotland — 'My last ten years I spent in North and South Wales,' wrote Jack Goodwin — but it was not the same, once crack mails burdened with up to twelve passengers instead of seven, horses broken-winded and slow. It was better, Corbett felt, to 'draw the veil over the decadence of a system which arrived nearer to perfection than any other road travel-ling . . . ever seen in the world'.

There is no record of coachmen finding work on the railway. A considerable number found employment on omnibuses. In London they congregated on the white omnibuses that ran from the West End to Richmond. They wore gold bands in their hats. Jack Brett, a guard on several southern coaches, was driving a bus in Sheffield in 1874. Billy Barratt, who had driven the Devonport–Taunton *Non Pareil*, finished up on the Devonport–Plymouth bus. Coachmen did not rush into bus work. It was 'too sudden a fall from their high estate, but many of them, as is sadly known, have been glad enough of 'bus patronage in later times'.[5]

They were fallen men; figures of fun. Some enjoyed seeing the imperious *jarveys* cut down to size. The '*reins* of these monarchs are at an end,' Alfred Crowquill crowed in 1843. Dickens, on another nostalgic excursion, visited an old coaching town (then, twenty years after its heyday, grovelling for a branch line). He was driven the seven miles to the Dolphin's Head by an old coachman. A cheeky young porter, hearing the destination, called sarcastically after the driver. 'All ri-ight! Don't hang yourself when you get there, Geo-o-rge!'[6]

One enthusiast, in 1874, thought he recognised the driver of a railway omnibus.

' ''Your face is very familiar to me,'' said I to an old chalked-off coachman.

' ''Maybe it is, sir; I drove the York Highflyer out of Stamford five-and-twenty years, and . . . should have been there now, if it wasn't for these tea-kettle flying engines, looking for all the world as if they were a-dragging a slice of Manchester or Birmingham after them.'' '[7]

Some coachmen went into inns, sometimes to decline with them, but some spent time in inns not their own trying to recapture the old days in alcoholic melancholia. Alfred Crowquill found one 'sulking away the fag-end of his existence in the privileged parlour of a little sporting house', still dressed

'Sulking away the fag-end of his existence': coachmen in decline.
British Library Newspaper Library

in coaching garb. 'A glass of brandy and water stood at his elbow, and he sighed as he observed my eyes directed towards the highly varnished representations of departed "fours" which adorned the walls.'

'Ah! Sir,' he addressed him, venting a profound sigh with pipe smoke, 'they'll never be seen again, 'cept in effigy! 'Twas a cruel consarn, sir, just as ve'd come to perfection, and beat the world, as I may say. Vy, ve changed on my "line" the whole "four", sir, in three minutes! Think o' that, sir; jist time to vipe the dust out o' my eyes, and off agin. A wonderful thing, sir; vy, I take it as our babbies' babbies, ven they sees them 'ere pictures, will never be persuaded as they vos real, but only allegaries! That 'ere vun with the four bays vos poor Bob Pointer's drag. He vos the man, to be sure, the best o' the werry best; but he's dead and gone, and lucky for him! For vot's the use of a man's living ven he hasn't got vun? He vos rather a fast 'un, 'cos he got among the nobs and the champagne, for he vos a first-rate. But, Lor' bless you! On'y to see that chap handle the lot; it vos a'most a miracle! No flourishing, but all together; not a flake o' sweat on vun horse more nor another; no firing o' minit guns out of his thong, for he never used his vip without a cause, but, by jingo! ven he *did* hit, he'd lift a hoss bang off his four legs! To see him handle the ribbins vos vat I call slap-up, and no mistake. No pulling here, nor pulling there; but Lor', he played 'em like a *pianner*; so dellikit yet firm that I do werily believe as he vould ha' driv four ladies without hurting a mouth of ere a vun on 'em?'[8]

So he went on . . . and on . . . .

It has frequently been implied that most coachmen and guards did not long outlive their calling but went into rapid decline. 'I fear the larger part died off rapidly,' surmised Edward Corbett. 'They were never a long-lived class of men . . . . The constant passing through the air promoted great appetites, which, for the most part, were fully gratified, and this, together with insufficient exercise, produced disease.' It was suggested coachmen were virtually unemployable in any other capacity. Captain Haworth reckoned that although 'coachmen and guards . . . were in receipt of comfortable incomes, it is very rare that an instance is found of their having provided for a rainy day'. Bill Harbridge, who had drawn £14–

£16 a week in fees on the Manchester mail, he mentions as
'another instance of the total want of prudence, unfortunately
so common to his class', for he died in the workhouse.

Jack Goodwin remembered differently. Harbridge first took
the Coach and Horses in Plymouth, afterwards drove a bus
from Putney to London Bridge for many years, and finally was
timekeeper for a steamboat company at Putney Bridge when he
died. Not quite so gloomy but no success story, and there were
others like it. Goodwin himself, after his last coach ceased to
run between Aberystwith and Oswestry, returned to Plymouth,
'but not, I am sorry to say, in ... easy circumstances ....
Many years ago I had a "tip" from off a coach, injuring my
spine, which was followed by a paralysis of the tongue, consequently I am unfit for an active life. I have for eight years
superintended a billiard room, in Old Town street, for Mr
Ramsden, Criteria Cigar Stores, George Street, Plymouth ...'
(The old guard could not resist one last opportunity to 'kick'
old passengers) '... where Queen's heads or post-office orders
would find — Jack Goodwin.' Then there was 'Poor Channen',
who retired into private life at Stoke, in good circumstances,
but became mentally deranged and threw himself off a railway
bridge.[9]

It is usual to complete accounts of coaching with such
stories along with that of Harry Little, who, when the railway
opened, said, 'Hang up my old whip over the fireplace. I shan't
want it never no more,' turned his face to the wall, and died.
Little Dick Vickers of the Holyhead mail hanged himself after
going bankrupt as a farmer, and Charles Holmes, of the *Old
Blenheim*, ended it all by jumping into the Thames.[10] These
tales conveniently write *finis* to a glorious age.

Such tragedies there were; decline and disappointment too,
but the majority seem to have realised the inevitability of it
all, swallowed their pride (sooner or later) and got on with
something else, often successfully. Their cheerful character
and fund of anecdotes made them good publicans. 'Smart Tom'
Pinner, a Birmingham–Cambridge coachman, took the Five
Ways Tavern, 'where he was well known and respected by
nearly everyone in Edgbaston'. George Wild, who had driven
the *Peveril of the Peak*, finally kept a pub in a village on the
Birmingham road. Guard Dan Olive took the Royal Oak, Ted-

dington, where he was always ready to 'spin some good old coaching yarn, also a tune on his old coaching bugle'.

Many gentleman coachmen had taken to the road for a 'bit of a lark' and simply returned to their place in society, although Sackville-Gwynne finished up as a Liverpool cabman. The men attracted to coaching in the 1820s and 1830s, who by their skill and responsibility had done much to improve its image, were not ones to curl up and die. Ben Holmes became and remained a respectable Birmingham retailer — of boots and shoes — with the 'same merry twinkle about the eye, the same hearty, cheery manner which made him so popular forty or fifty years ago ... and the same deferential, yet self-respecting, manner'. Bill Tolly stuck with coaches to the end. After the *Erin-go-bragh* he took the Worcester mail, the Holyhead and then the Ludlow coach, before becoming a successful omnibus and car proprietor in Hockley.[12] Richard Glover also stayed as long as he could, driving the mail from Oxford to Cheltenham until 1861, when he started farming and kept a livery stable in Cheltenham. Not a few kept their connection with horses, as jobbers, livery stable keepers, and dealers. John Hex, Exeter *Subscription* guard, was, in 1874, tenant on an extensive farm of Sir Maney Lopes. Barton, driver on the Birmingham and Dover roads, became a veterinary surgeon. Tom Holtby, the one-time post boy, far from having put nothing away, was able to dabble in a variety of lines (more as a hobby than from necessity), most of which lost him a fair amount of money, but he still left £3,000 when he died in 1863 aged seventy-two.[13]

The idea that the majority died unusually young is probably something of a myth. Many were still around in the 1860s and 1870s. A photograph of 1883 shows William Snowdon, who drove the Oxford–Cheltenham coach, aged seventy-seven, Newman Glover, who drove the Chester mail, aged seventy-four, and his brother Richard, aged seventy-nine. He lived to be ninety. Frank Wragg died in 1891 at eighty-five, William Clement of the Canterbury–London *Tally-ho* at ninety-one and Harry Ward aged seventy-eight in 1892. Thomas Packer, many years on the Bath–Cheltenham road, died in 1874 at eighty-four. Philip 'Tim' Carter of the London–Brighton *Red Rover* was eighty-eight when he died in 1893. John Mallis, who

Three old coachmen. *Left to right*: William Snowdon, seventy-seven; Newman Glover, seventy-four; Richard Glover, seventy-nine

drove the *Royal Sovereign* from Brighton to Windsor, was still living in Brighton in 1893 aged eighty-four. Matty Marsh died at ninety-four. Thomas Layfield, 'a steady man, well respected by all classes, and looked up to by the nobility and gentry as being an upright and trustworthy coachman' in Yorkshire, was eighty-one when he died in 1882.[14] There were many more.

And what of those noble pillars of town and establishment — proprietors and innkeepers? Several of the largest proprietors went in with the railways as directors and shareholders,

Chaplin (later chairman of the London & South Western Railway) and Horne were two. They joined forces as carriers for the London & Birmingham Railway in conjunction with some provincial proprietors like Matthew Outhwaite of Leeds, and as well as dealing with freight from Camden Town they ran omnibuses from Euston station and between Paddington and Nine Elms. Nelson's too, went into omnibuses. Sherman became a carrier for the Great Western (after standing out some time against the London & Birmingham Railway by running a day and night coach, with little success). Other provincial proprietors went in with the railways, like Brotherton and Waddell in Birmingham. At a humbler level 'Tommy' Cooper, a proprietor at Thatcham near Newbury, finished up as the 'courteous and obliging' stationmaster on the LSWR at Richmond.[15]

If a few proprietors challenged the railways head-on, to fail miserably, most were either bought off or simply gave up ignominiously. In Ireland Bianconi, despite his Latin temperament, remained calm. Rather than dissipating his energies and finances, he resisted all invitations to oppose any lines. At an opposition meeting in Dublin he listened for a time and finally said, 'I think I know as much of the country as any gentleman in this room, and I look upon it to be as foolish to try to prevent the establishment of railways as to try to stem the Liffey. My own loss . . . would be greater than . . . the combined losses of all . . . here present. Still I see that railways must be made and I not only do not oppose them, but I have taken shares in the undertakings.' Their growth did force him to discontinue running cars over 4,534 miles of road between 1846 and 1865, but during the same period he extended over another 3,594 miles. He was not too proud, as railways broke up his great lines, to run cars to meet trains at stations. It was still more than a viable concern when he began, in 1865, to sell it off liberally to men who had run it so faithfully for him. Passenger traffic in 1864 still realised £27,731 and mail contracts £12,000. Could British proprietors not have done the same?

This may be to ignore differences between Irish and British transport. Irish proprietors had not struggled under a heavy and increasingly unfair tax system. Cars were more flexible and cheaper than coaches (although the British could have introduced more economic vehicles). The British system was much more fragmented in ownership and organisation. Not least, most proprietors did not own the vehicles they operated. Equally, the inns, the foundation of the British system, became something of a millstone. Bianconi owned no inns. His plan was to rent large premises, reserving to himself outer yards, stables and corn storage, sub-letting the main houses, which he converted into hotels for his agents. He simply charged them what he paid his landlord. In this way his property was protected from all risks. Bianconi was first and foremost a transport man, whereas many British proprietors were not.

The Irish system was also less developed than the British, so there was still scope for expansion even after the railways. But the abrupt ending of the British coach system, with the main railway lines barely built, did leave a real and serious transport vacuum in areas untouched by railways for many years. As early as 1840 the *Times* had come to 'understand that on the old line of road from Liverpool to Manchester via Warrington there is not a solitary coach to be seen. If a man of business at Liverpool have business at Prescot . . . and . . . wishes to get to Warrington, he [has] no choice but to walk, there being neither horse nor vehicle in the town licensed to let out to hire.'[16]

It was to become a national problem. As W. Pennell, a Midland Poor Law Commissioner, remarked in 1842, 'the railroads have driven the coaches . . . off the roads, running at right angles with them, as well as parallel; and persons travelling short journeys, or those taking long journeys from and to places in planes lying at right angles with the railroads are deprived of those facilities which they formerly had'.[17]

It was a situation ripe for exploitation, but it was an opportunity generally missed by British proprietors and taken by others using omnibuses much later. Had proprietors been more adaptable, although there would have been less glory and probably reduced incomes, they might have saved more from the wreckage. Perhaps it was a case of glory or nothing. Most preferred to go while they were still ahead.

Some innkeepers carried on and managed to survive reasonably well, for in many towns the chief coaching inns had, like the White Hart at Aylesbury, catered for banquets, weekly

'Bianconi owned no inns.' He rented them and sub-let them to his
agents. Preparing cars at Dan Hearn's hotel, Clonmel, and . . .

. . . arriving at Commin's Hotel, Waterford. *Both British Library*

dinners, election meetings, weddings, the assizes. The White Hart was patronised by 'the most glittering high society of aristocratic huntsmen and sportsmen' who came down from London. They still came after the railway opened in 1839. But all this was gilt on the gingerbread — which was the passing post and coach trade. Samuel Griffiths of the Star and Angel inns, Oxford, in 1837, reckoned two-thirds of his business depended on passing trade.[18]

Some sold out to concentrate on their farms. The elder John Fowler began to diversify in 1837, becoming tenant of Broughton Farm, where he later retired, leaving his son in charge of the White Hart. But emasculation of coaching and posting had taken the bread-and-butter out of the business, and in 1853 he entered the tenancy of Prebendal Farm, near Aylesbury, selling the White Hart soon after. Fowler went on to become a successful farmer, breeder and publicist for British agriculture, travelling widely, especially to shows at home and abroad. He also became director of a railway company.

Owners of isolated road houses were hard hit, if they carried on, but most cut their losses to realise some capital by selling. Tom Bradley showed how many inns reverted to use as mansions, manor and farm houses. The Castle at Marlborough, 'an extremely stately and exclusive' inn, had originally been the country seat of the Marquess of Hertford. Ruined by railways, and long empty, it eventually became the nucleus of Marlborough College. The Bull's Head, later Royal Sussex, Hotel on the Holyhead road, once the seat of Sir Clement Fisher of Packington, reverted to a private residence as Darleston Hall.[19]

Inns in villages and small towns, especially those by-passed by the railways, were hardest hit. Rarely could they be put to any other use on such a grand scale. Some were converted into shops, the stables into cottages. Otherwise they died by degrees and the town died with them.

Already by 1843, Crowquill found, 'weeds encroach upon the once frequented ways; long rows of once commodious ''stabling'' are dark, still and untenanted; the neglected doors fall down from their hinges; the grand old inn, the heart and vitality of the place, stands a cheerless ruin, and the moss grows upon its never-trodden steps'.[20]

Some years later Grantley Berkeley revisited the Anchor at Liphook. It survived, but only just. He found the stables a 'melancholy sight' and 'the whole thing given up to dreary desolation' ...; 'no smart waiter, with a white napkin whisked round his thumb, came forth to my summons, the few people in the house looked like broken-down farming men and women ...'. His dinner was no tender fowl, selected and hung as in the old days, but 'a poor dear old chuckie, seated at roost in all her feathers', pulled 'screaming from her perch' not an hour before, to be served 'tough to table'.[21]

Lord William Pitt Lennox found 'Nothing is now so forlorn as a great rambling, half-aired, half-appointed country inn; waiter acting boots, boots acting post-boy, or maybe all three; and cook acting chambermaid, barmaid and all'.[22]

Dickens, when he went down memory lane around 1860, illustrated graphically how the railways had devastated these old coaching towns and the road industry generally. He found the once famous New White Hart with whitewashed windows and boarded-up door. It had last been occupied by the Literary Institution. The whole town was decaying — 'Most of the harness makers and corn dealers were gone the way of the coaches ...', and business among the remaining tradesmen was 'bitter bad'. One grizzled old coachmaker soldiered on, 'a soured man and a discontented'. The turnpike keeper was reduced to cobbling, his wife to selling ginger-beer and sweets.

'How goes turnpike business, master?' Dickens enquired as he repaired a shoe in the toll house porch.

'It don't go at all, master. It's stopped.'

Near by, Dickens met a grumpy old post boy breaking stones, so reduced in circumstances as to be living in the 'po-shay' (post-chaise) decaying in a vegetable allotment.

The Dolphin's Head survived — but only just: it was 'dying by inches' and 'everywhere expressed past coachfulness and present coachlessness'. The coloured prints of coaching scenes were discoloured and moth-eaten, hanging askew. The anchovy sauce had 'turned blue some years ago'.

Bustling porters, boots, ostlers, waiters were now represented by 'a mournful young woman with one eye susceptible of guidance, and one uncontrollable eye; which latter

The end. *British Library Newspaper Library*

seeming to wander, in quest of stage coaches, deepened the melancholy . . .'.

We can only guess where ancillary staff disappeared to. Some no doubt died with their inns, others perhaps moved to work on the railways, perhaps in railway hotels. Possibly proprietors' farms absorbed a few. For all, the demise of coaches was a salutary and sad shock, although most probably took it better than the horsekeeper at Storrington. He had been heard to lament the decay of coaching, then came to believe he had something growing inside him. Both matters preyed upon his mind, and one day, after harnessing his horses, he went and hanged himself.[23]

The Dolphin's Head was sorely shrunken. Half the bar was a tobacco shop, and the 'once glorious yard' had been taken over by a 'scientific shoeing smith and veterinary surgeon', a jobber occupied part of the extensive stables, and another part had been turned into a chapel, a wheelwright's shop and a Young Men's Mutual Improvement and Discussion Society. The innkeeper, J. Mellows, 'having so little to do, was habitually thrown back on his internal resources — by which I mean the Dolphin's cellar'.[24] Such was the graveyard of the Coaching Age, if not necessarily of the people who had once worked in it.

NOTES

The following abbreviations have been used: HC or HL, House of Commons or Lords; HLRO, House of Lords Record Office; Lib., Reference Library; LRO, Lancashire County Record Office; NRO, Northamptonshire County Record Office; SC, Select Committee.

Chapter 1
PET AND DARLING OF THE PEOPLE

1 J. K. Fowler, *Records of Old Times*, 1898, 120–1
2 William Bayzand, 'Coaching in and out of Oxford, 1820–40', *Oxford Historical Society Journal*, xxxxvii, 1905, 265–309
3 *Times*, 15 October 1831, 25 August 1820, 22 August 1829
4 B. Blackmantle and R. Cruikshank, *The English Spy*, II, 1826, 340
5 M. E. Haworth, *Road Scrapings*, 1882, 137
6 T. Bradley, *The Old Coaching Days in Yorkshire*, 1889, 64
7 J. K. Fowler, *Recollections of Old Country Life*, 1894, 89–91
8 *Leisure Hour*, 1874, 503
9 H. J. Hart, *Coaching and Tourist Guide of Warwickshire, c.* 1885, 18, Birmingham Lib.
10 H. Smail, *Coaching Times and After*, 1948, 67
11 Miss Weeton, *Journal of a Governess, 1811–25*, ed. Edward Hall, Oxford University Press, 1939, 56
12 *Land and Water*, 3 April 1875
13 J. T. Slugg, *Reminiscences of Manchester Fifty Years Ago*, 1881, 218
14 V. A. Wilson, *The Coaching Era*, 1922, 80
15 *Land and Water*, 19 December 1874
16 M. J. O'Connell, *Charles Bianconi, A Biography*, 1878, 139. Subsequent details of Irish coaching practice are drawn from this source unless indicated otherwise
17 *Land and Water*, 22 August 1874
18 *Ibid*, 2 January 1875

19   E. Corbett, *An Old Coachman's Chatter*, 1890, 45
20   S. Harris ('An Old Stager'), *Old Coaching Days*, 1882, 265–6
21   J. Hissey, *On the Box Seat*, 1886, 232
22   *Land and Water*, 26 December 1874; Harris, 266
23   B. Austen, 'The impact of the mail coach on public coach services in England and Wales, 1784–1840', *Journal of Transport History*, II, No. 1, March 1981, 34
24   *Census of Great Britain, 1851, Population Tables*, II, Pt. 1 (1854) [1691–1], p. cxxii
25   G. N. Goodwin, *Green Lanes of Hampshire, Surrey and Sussex*, 1882, 117
26   Lord William Pitt Lennox, *Coaching and Anecdotes of the Road*, 1876, 59–60
27   *Illustrated London News*, 5 April 1845, 213; O'Connell, 80, 78, 51, 59
28   G. F. Berkeley, *My Life and Recollections*, 1865, 268

Chapter 2
A SERIOUS PENANCE

1   W. Wilson, *Coaching Past and Present*, 1885, 23
2   R. A. H. Spiers, *Coaching Days in Oxford and at the Mitre*, 1928, 46; Bayzand, 301
3   H. Williams, *Stage Coaches in Wales*, Williams, Barry, 1977, 15
4   C. Dickens, *Sketches by Boz*, Oxford University Press, 1969 edn., 132
5   *Times*, 29 October 1824
6   W. O. Tristram, *Coaching Days and Coaching Ways*, 1931 edn., 99–100
7   *Times*, 23 and 26 August 1828
8   *Ibid.*, 11 June 1822
9   Baron d'Haussez, *Great Britain in 1833*, 1833, 71
10   Lord W. P. Lennox, *My Recollections*, I, 1874, 118–19
11   Sir George Head, *A Home Tour through the Manufacturing Districts*, 1836; 1968, 114–15
12   *Times*, 27 October 1824, 20 September 1825, 21 September 1837
13   J. W. Hyde, *A Hundred Years by Post*, 1891, 64
14   Bayzand, 282, 293–4
15   C. Dickens, *The Uncommercial Traveller*, Oxford University Press, 1963 edn., 243
16   Fowler, *Recollections*, 10–11
17   Lord W. P. Lennox, *Coaching*, 1876, 94; *My Recollections*, I, 125
18   Nimrod, *My Horses, and other Essays*, ed. E. D. Cuming, 1928, 237
19   *Times*, 27 March 1835
20   *Land and Water*, 5 June 1875

21 C. G. Harper, *Historic and Picturesque Inns of Old England*, 1926, 9–10
22 *Railway Times*, 1838, 611–12

Chapter 3
LOW FELLOWS

1 *Manchester Guardian*, 8 September 1847; V. A. Wilson, 16
2 Bayzand, 300–1
3 Nimrod, 195
4 d'Haussez, 69
5 Bayzand, 292
6 *Land and Water*, 20 February 1875
7 W. Wilson, 23–4
8 Berkeley, *My Life*, I, 267–9
9 Blackmantle, 129–30
10 *Land and Water*, 26 December 1874
11 *Times*, 6 August 1832
12 Duke of Beaufort, *Driving*, 1894 edn., 228
13 *Times*, 27 December 1826
14 *SC on the Observance of the Sabbath Day*, 1831–32 (697), VIII, qq. 1902, 2011
15 *SC on Postage*, HC 658, 1837–38, xx–II, q. 10224
16 *Times*, 22 June 1836
17 Hart, 22; *Land and Water*, 1 August 1874
18 Bradley, 203
19 Hyde, 62–3
20 Harris, 219
21 Bayzand, 286
22 *Times*, 13 September 1834
23 *Ibid.*, 17 August 1827

Chapter 4
HALF-SEAS-OVER

1 W. C. A. Blew, *Brighton and its Coaches*, 1894, 267
2 *Times*, 6 August 1832
3 *SC on Drunkenness*, 1834 (559), VIII, q. 317
4 *Land and Water*, 25 July 1874
5 *Times*, 27 June 1823, 24 November 1827
6 Williams, 11; *Times*, 30 June 1837
7 M. J. Nobbs, *Old Coaching Days*, 1892, 22
8 T. Cross, *Autobiography of a Stage Coachman*, II, 1861, 150–4
9 *Times*, 18 October 1825
10 *Railway Times*, 1838, 120
11 *SC on Postage*, 1837–8, qq. 10173–6
12 *Report of the Commissioners for Management of the Post Office* (*Post Office Commission, 1835*) HC 313, 1835, xlviii, p. 76

13 *Times*, 1 September 1818
14 J. W. Hyde, *The Royal Mail*, 1885, 60–1
15 *Times*, 4 August 1823; *York Herald*, 27 March 1824
16 *Coventry Herald*, 9 April 1830
17 *Times*, 16 August 1827
18 *Ibid.*, 1 December 1827
19 *Ibid.*, 22 October 1838
20 *York Herald*, 21 August 1824
21 *Ibid.*, 3 April 1824
22 *Times*, 15 September 1827
23 *Ibid.*, 9 August 1838
24 Bradley, 163
25 *Land and Water*, 14 November, 25 July, 7 November 1874; Nimrod, 188
26 *Coventry Herald*, 9 April 1830
27 *Times*, 24 July 1838

Chapter 5
CUTTERS AND CADS

1 T. C. Barker and and M. Robbins, *A History of London Transport*, I, Allen & Unwin, 1975, 5
2 *Times*, 27 July, 13 July 1822. Sources for this chapter are from the *Times* unless indicated otherwise
3 3 February 1825
4 8 November 1825
5 10 May, 10 August 1826, 1 June 1827
6 24 December 1827, 8 November 1826, 15 November 1825
7 4 December 1822
8 13 September 1831; Captain Malet, *Annals of the Road*, 1876, 64–6
9 7 June 1824
10 17 November 1825
11 10 August 1826
12 17 February 1832
13 15 January 1834
14 12 August 1835
15 Dickens, *Boz*, 139
16 23 September 1836, 18 March 1840
17 21 October, 20 September 1836, 14 October 1834
18 7 November 1834
19 10 October 1839, 24 October 1836, 14 August 1838, 22 May 1839
20 18 April, 26 April 1839
21 29 October 1834
22 2, 3 February 1836
23 15 October 1835, 14 October 1834, 29 January 1831
24 13 September 1831, 26 January 1837
25 16 March 1835

Chapter 6
DELAY, EXTORTION AND HIGHWAYMEN

1 Bayzand, 300–1, 291
2 W. Potts, *Banbury in the Coaching Days*, 1929, 26
3 London and Birmingham Railway Bill, HL 2 July 1832, 97, 87, HLRO
4 *Times*, 21 January 1822
5 *Ibid.*, 27 November 1822
6 *Ibid.*, 8 August 1833
7 *Ibid.*, 4 October 1822; A. Groom, *Old London Coaching Inns*, 1928, 36–7
8 *Times*, 20 November 1838
9 *Ibid.*, 2 September 1837, 27 November 1822; *Sessions Papers*, PCOM 1/19, 1823, 153, PRO
10 *Times*, 7, 15, 21 October 1818
11 *Ibid.*, 14 January 1823, 2 November 1825
12 *Railway Times*, 1838, 612; *Times*, 7 October 1818, 21 January 1822
13 *Times*, 18 June 1830
14 Blew, 220–1, 267
15 *Times*, 28 January 1837; *Land and Water*, 9 January 1875
16 *Times*, 29 October 1824
17 *Manchester Mercury*, 20 February 1821
18 *Manchester Guardian*, 12 and 15 November 1845
19 *Times*, 26 November 1822, 24 September 1818, 29 December 1838
20 *Ibid.*, 17 December 1822, 14 October 1818
21 *Times*, 14 April 1823, 24 April 1824, 2 April 1822; *Cork Southern Reporter*, 3 February 1827; *Times*, 15 December 1827

Chapter 7
THE SWELL MOB

1 *Times*, 22 November 1825; Blew, 163; *Session Papers*, 1815–16, PCOM 1/12 10, 121
2 Blew, 141; *Times*, 1 December 1827, 30 October 1828
3 *The Memoirs of James Hardy Vaux, by Himself*, ed. N. McLachlan, 1819; 1964, Heineman, 142–3
4 *Times*, 14 January 1823, 12 January 1820, 20 January 1824, 9 February 1825, 25 December 1824
5 *Ibid.*, 24 February 1825, 20 September, 4 October, 27 November 1822
6 *Ibid.*, 14 December 1822, 30 November 1827
7 *Ibid.*, 24 February 1825, 17 December 1822; PCOM 1/19, 1823, 150–3, PRO
8 Hyde, *A Hundred Years by Post*, 72
9 PCOM 1/12, 1816, 154–5, PRO

10 *Times*, 24 December 1818, 17 November 1823
11 PCOM 1/21, 1825, 106, PRO
12 *Times*, 17 November 1822
13 *Ibid.*, 10 February 1830
14 *Ibid.*, 30 March, 29 April 1831
15 *Ibid.*, 30 March 1835
16 *Ibid.*, 14 October 1839
17 *Ibid.*, 14 January 1823
18 *Coventry Herald*, 2 April 1830

Chapter 8
A VERY QUEER LOT

1 *Times*, 16 September 1836
2 *Ibid.*, 17 November 1836
3 *Ibid.*, 28 October 1831, 8 August 1828, 17 December 1827
4 *Ibid.*, 7 October 1836, 21 February 1838
5 *Ibid.*, 8 November 1834, 10 August 1839, 7 November 1825
6 *Ibid.*, 22 September 1829, 17 December 1827
7 *Ibid.*, 14 September 1836
8 *Post Office Commission*, 1835, p. 41
9 *Times*, 1 September 1818, 30 June 1837, 20 August 1838
10 Beaufort, 242, 223
11 *York Herald*, 21 August 1824; *Times*, 16 October 1833
12 *Times*, 16 July 1830
13 *Ibid.*, 19 October 1833, 11 August 1828, 4 January 1830
14 *Manchester Mercury*, 6 August 1821; *Times*, 3 April 1840; Blew, 164
15 *Times*, 15 September 1829; Blew, 184
16 *Times*, 15 September 1827
17 *Land and Water*, 10 October 1874
18 Howarth, 76–7
19 *Times*, 13 July 1825, 11 May 1836
20 Harris, 125–7
21 *Post Office Commission*, 1835, p. 44; *Land and Water*, 14 November 1874; *Railway Times*, 1838, 153
22 Bayzand, 272–6
23 W. Wilson, 13; *SC on Postage*, 1838, qq. 10214–15, 10216
24 *Times*, 15 August 1837

Chapter 9
IT WAS INDEED MISERY

1 *Railway Times*, 1838, 47, 120, 153
2 *Times*, 11 December 1822
3 *Times*, 14 September 1829
4 *Ibid.*, 15 February 1831

5 *Railway Times*, 1838, 688; *Times*, 14 December 1822, 20 November 1833
6 Harris, 267–9
7 *SC on Postage*, 1838, qq. 10153–7; *Times*, 22 January 1838; C. Cahill, *Anecdotes and Reminiscences*, 1892, 21
8 *Manchester Mercury*, 23 January 1821
9 *Railway Times*, 1838, 153; *Times*, 23 January 1823
10 Hyde, *A Hundred Years by Post*, 46
11 Subsequent details are based on reports in the *Times*, 27 December 1836 to 3 January 1837
12 *Land and Water*, 8 August 1874
13 Goodwin, 13–14

Chapter 10
PECULIAR TO THEMSELVES

1 *SC on Drunkenness*, 1834, q. 317
2 *Quarterley Review*, LIX, 1837, 326
3 Slugg, 216
4 Reynardson, 11–12; *SC on Observance of the Sabbath*, 1832, q. 2031
5 *Land and Water*, 8 August, 28 March 1874; Nobbs, 49
6 *Illustrated London News*, 22 February 1845, 123; Blew, 131
7 Haworth, 76–8
8 *Times*, 7 January 1833; Blew, 246; Cross, II, 71
9 *Land and Water*, 4, 11 April 1874
10 Corbett, 175; *SC on Observance of the Sabbath*, 1832, q. 2030; Slugg, 216, 212, 215
11 *Times*, 16 February 1827
12 *Ibid.*, 30 October 1828; Hart, 22–4
13 *SC on Railroad Communication*, 1837–8 (257), XVI, q. 1179
14 Slugg, 213; Corbett, 175; Blew, 265
15 *Land and Water*, 25 July 1874
16 Hart, 22–4
17 *Land and Water*, 11 April 1874
18 Beaufort, 172
19 Hart, 18, 20–2; *Land and Water*, 22 August 1874
20 Smail, 65; Bradley, 15
21 *Times*, 6 August 1832; Nobbs, 50
22 Beaufort, 179; *Times*, 27 October 1838
23 PCOM 1/19, 1823, 150, PRO; *Land and Water*, 25 July 1874
24 *Illustrated London News*, 29 June 1844, 409
25 Blew, 204
26 Salt, *Statistics and Calculations*, 1845, 83
27 Butcher (Daventry) 14/3; PSJ 225/40; 338 p/Th 43, NRO
28 *Post Office Commission*, 1835, 73–7
29 *Times*, 16 August 1827; Bradley, 29, 129, 88, 68, 51; Goodwin, 119–20; Fowler, *Records*, 106
30 PSJ 255/12, NRO

Chapter 11
DIFFERENT TEMPERS TO PLEASE

1 Haworth, 129–30; *SC on Postage*, 1837–8, q. 10227
2 *Coventry Herald*, 9 April 1830
3 Beaufort, 226, 212; *Land and Water*, 4 April 1874
4 Slugg, 217
5 PCOM 1/19, 1823, 153, PRO
6 *Times*, 16 February 1827
7 *Land and Water*, 19 September 1874; Reynardson, 194–5
8 *Times*, 30 August 1839
9 *Ibid.*, 16 July 1830; Nimrod, 161–2
10 *Times*, 23 October 1832, 20 September 1822, 7 October 1823, 20 January 1824
11 Blew, 29, 142–4, 155–6; *Times*, 27 August 1827, 22 August 1823, 23 October 1832
12 *Ibid.*, 25 October 1824
13 *Land and Water*, 27 June 1874
14 *Coventry Herald*, 2 April 1830
15 *Times*, 3 January 1840
16 *Ibid.*, 13 August 1834, 28 July 1829
17 *Ibid.*, 30 October 1834, 11 January 1837
18 *Ibid.*, 17 December 1827, 24 April 1824, 16 February 1827
19 *Ibid.*, 26 January 1838; Hart, 26
20 *Brighton Gazette*, 30 January 1838; *Times*, 15 March 1839, 21 November 1837, 17 November 1836
21 *Times*, 20 July 1837, 3 April 1840, 13 August 1834, 25 August 1828; Hyde, *A Hundred Years by Post*, 71

Chapter 12
FOR THE SAKE OF PUTTING THEM ON

1 *Times*, 11 April 1823, 27 August, 8 August 1828
2 Salt, 83
3 *Post Office Commission*, 1835, p. 38; *SC on Taxation on Internal Communication (SC on Taxation, 1837)*, 1837 (456), XX, q. 54
4 *Post Office Commission*, 1835, p. 23
5 *Times*, 19 April 1824
6 *Times*, 22 October 1821; Bradley, 68, 76, 47; PCOM 1/23, 1826, 46, PRO
7 Smail, 112; *Land and Water*, 5 June 1875
8 Beaufort, 230; Smail, 65
9 *Post Office Commission*, 1835, 79. 78; London and Birmingham Railway Bill, HL, 29 June 1832, pp. 30–1, HLRO
10 *SC on Taxation*, 1837, qq. 481, 455
11 *Ibid.*, 480; Bradley, 125–7; Blew, 134–7, 146
12 *Post Office Commission*, 1835, p. 41
13 Fowler, *Echoes of old Country Life*, 1892, 220, 218
14 *Post Office Commission*, 1835, 41

15 *Ibid.*, 1835, p. 44; O'Connell, 73
16 *SC on Taxation*, 1837, p. 24; *Post Office Commission*, p. 38
17 *City Press*, 29 September 1866; F. E. Baines, *On the Track of the Mail Coach*, 1895, 30
18 *Land and Water*, 4 April 1874; E. Edwards, *The Old Taverns of Birmingham*, 1879, 89–90
19 *Dictionary of National Biography*, 461; *Illustrated London News*, 5 April 1845; *SC on Postage*, 1838, qq. 10153–7; O'Connell
20 Bradley, 30–1
21 Groom, 5, 14; Cross I, 113; V. A. Wilson, 109; A. Maudslay, *Highways and Horses*, 1888, 130; Edwards, 90
22 *Land and Water*, 4 April 1874; Bradley, 191–2
23 *Times*, 19 June 1839; Fowler, *Records*, 16
24 *SC on Taxation*, 1837, 352, 472
25 *York Herald*, 3 April 1824

Chapter 13
HORSES NOR WHIPS SPARED

1 *Times*, 21 January 1834. Unless otherwise indicated, details of comparative practice have been drawn from: Nimrod (C. J. Apperley), *My Horses, and other Essays*, ed. E. D. Cuming, 1928, 229–44; Baron d'Haussez, *Great Britain in 1833*, 69–91; Duke of Beaufort, *Driving*, 1889; 1894, 320–9, 355–8; C. Dickens, *American Notes*, 1957, OUP, 131–2, 189
2 *Illustrated London News*, 25 November 1843, 340
3 *Manchester Guardian*, 21 October 1840
4 *Land and Water*, 10 April 1875
5 *Ibid.*, 24 April 1875
6 Fowler, *Records*, 118, 113
7 J. Mottershead, *The Traveller's Guide*, 1827, 87
8 *Land and Water*, 3 April 1875
9 *Ibid.*, 7 November 1874

Chapter 14
RASH TOM, LITTLE BALL AND SPICEY JACK

1 Haworth, 35
2 *Times*, 26 December 1822
3 Nobbs, 52
4 *Times*, 16 October 1822, 14 February 1820
5 *Ibid.*, 2 December 1825
6 *Land and Water*, 10 October 1874
7 *Times*, 8 October 1834
8 *Ibid.*, 20 January 1836
9 Cahill, 53
10 *Jackson's Oxford Journal*, 19 October 1816
11 *Times*, 4, 5 August 1825

12 *Ibid.*, 13 January 1836
13 W. Wilson, 21–3
14 *Times*, 4 September 1837, 9 November 1829
15 *Illustrated London News*, 28 January 1843
16 Bayzand, 286, 301
17 Beaufort, 173, 183, 206
18 *Land and Water*, 14 November 1874
19 Hart, 22
20 E. Edwards, *Personal Recollections of Birmingham*, 1877, 1
21 K. A. Austin, *The Lights of Cobb and Co.*, Rigby, Adelaide, 1967, 149–50

Chapter 15
DYING BY INCHES

1 *Times*, 10 August 1832
2 *SC on Railroad Communication*, 1838, qq. 1396–465
3 *Boz*, 687
4 *Times*, 26 May 1840
5 Blew, 228; *Land and Water*, 20 June, 26 December 1874
6 *The Uncommercial Traveller*, 242
7 *Land and Water*, 30 January 1875
8 *Illustrated London News*, 28 January 1843, 52–3
9 *Land and Water*, 18 April, 20 June 1874
10 D. Mountfield, *The Coaching Age*, Robert Hale, 1976, 175
11 Hart, 26; *Land and Water*, 7 November, 25 July 1874
12 Hart, 19–20, 24
13 Smail, 107; *Land and Water*, 20 June 1874; Malet, 155; Bradley, 70–1
14 Smail, 106, 107, 109, 112; Nobbs, 53; *Land and Water*, 12 December 1874; Blew, 161, 297; Bradley, 107; *World Newspaper*, 11 July 1888
15 *Land and Water*, 28 November 1874, 9 January 1875, 7 November 1874; Barker and Harris, 40
16 *Times*, 1 May 1840
17 *SC on Railways*, 1844, 318, XI, p. 47
18 Oxford and Great Western Railway Bill, HC, 15 March 1837, p. 6
19 C. G. Harper, *Historic Inns*, 117–18; *The Old Cross*, August 1878, Birmingham Lib.
20 *Illustrated London News*, 28 January 1843, 53
21 Berkeley, *Anecdotes of the upper Ten Thousand*, I, 1867, 104–5
22 Lennox, *Coaching*, 219
23 Blew, 241
24 *The Uncommercial Traveller*, 241–8

INDEX

Numbers in italics indicate illustrations